Well Diary...I Have Tuberculosis

Researching a Teenager's 1918 Sanatorium Experience

Shirley Morgan

Dedication

This work is dedicated in memory of Janet Parker Decker who protected the diary of Evelyn Bellak within the Adirondack Research Room of the Saranac Lake Free Library and shared with me her curiosity about Evelyn.

Published by the Author
Copyright © 2014 by Shirley Morgan
All rights reserved.
ISBN-13: 978-1493563043
ISBN-10: 1493563041
LCCN: 2014906646

Front cover photographs: top and bottom, courtesy of the Saranac Lake Free Library; center, courtesy of Helen Ryan Garlock. Back cover photographs: top, courtesy of Helen Ryan Garlock; bottom, courtesy of Patricia Powers.
Title page photograph courtesy of Helen Ryan Garlock.

Table of Contents

What Research Revealed

Introduction to The Diary

Author photograph

A modest, worn-looking diary that I discovered in my local library begins: *Well, Diary, I'll introduce myself. My name is Evelyn. I'm 16 years old. I have tuberculosis and at the present time am in the Ray Brook Sanitarium trying to get cured and you must keep my secrets for I'll tell you things that I want no one to know.* Tuberculosis was a devastating diagnosis for anyone at the time of the first entry in the small diary: January 1, 1918. Having tuberculosis meant that you had to face the possibility that you would die from it. Without doubt, Evelyn had known many people who had died from the disease. And she was not the only person in her family who was suffering from tuberculosis. What must it have been like, so long ago, to be very sick, confined to a hospital with a disease for which there was no reliable cure at the time, and to be just sixteen years old?

The little brown book in the library has a hand-written title: "FOND MEMORIES OF RAY BROOK" on the front cover. Inside, it is signed: *Evelyn Bellak*, and inscribed: *To Evelyn from Maidy. A Merry Christmas & a Scrumptious New Year. Xmas 1917.* Evidently, Evelyn had received the blank diary as a gift. She wrote in it faithfully, recording the events of every day during a portion of her stay at the Ray Brook State Hospital for the treatment of tuberculosis, located in Essex County, New York. What Evelyn records in her diary is a moving account of her mostly spirited, yet sometimes downhearted, undertaking of the "rest cure" for tuberculosis in the era before drugs were developed to treat the disease.

CALENDAR 1918.

	Sun.	Mon.	Tue.	Wed.	Thurs.	Fri.	Sat.		Sun.	Mon.	Tue.	Wed.	Thurs.	Fri.	Sat.
JAN.	..	..	1	2	3	4	5	JULY	..	1	2	3	4	5	6
	6	7	8	9	10	11	12		7	8	9	10	11	12	13
	13	14	15	16	17	18	19		14	15	16	17	18	19	20
	20	21	22	23	24	25	26		21	22	23	24	25	26	27
	27	28	29	30	31	..	..		28	29	30	31	..	..	..
FEB.	..	..	..	..	..	1	2	AUG.	..	..	..	..	1	2	3
	3	4	5	6	7	8	9		4	5	6	7	8	9	10
	10	11	12	13	14	15	16		11	12	13	14	15	16	17
	17	18	19	20	21	22	23		18	19	20	21	22	23	24
	24	25	26	27	28	..	..		25	26	27	28	29	30	31
MAR.	..	..	..	..	..	1	2	SEPT.	1	2	3	4	5	6	7
	3	4	5	6	7	8	9		8	9	10	11	12	13	14
	10	11	12	13	14	15	16		15	16	17	18	19	20	21
	17	18	19	20	21	22	23		22	23	24	25	26	27	28
	24	25	26	27	28	29	30		29	30	..	..	..	..	..
	31	..	..	..	..	..	..								
APRIL.	..	1	2	3	4	5	6	OCT.	..	..	1	2	3	4	5
	7	8	9	10	11	12	13		6	7	8	9	10	11	12
	14	15	16	17	18	19	20		13	14	15	16	17	18	19
	21	22	23	24	25	26	27		20	21	22	23	24	25	26
	28	29	30	..	..	..	..		27	28	29	30	31	..	..
MAY.	..	..	..	1	2	3	4	NOV.	..	..	..	..	..	1	2
	5	6	7	8	9	10	11		3	4	5	6	7	8	9
	12	13	14	15	16	17	18		10	11	12	13	14	15	16
	19	20	21	22	23	24	25		17	18	19	20	21	22	23
	26	27	28	29	30	31	..		24	25	26	27	28	29	30
JUNE.	..	..	..	..	..	..	1	DEC.	1	2	3	4	5	6	7
	2	3	4	5	6	7	8		8	9	10	11	12	13	14
	9	10	11	12	13	14	15		15	16	17	18	19	20	21
	16	17	18	19	20	21	22		22	23	24	25	26	27	28
	23	24	25	26	27	28	29		29	30	31	..	..	..	..
	30	..	..	..	..	..	..								

THE

NATIONAL

DIARY

NATIONAL

1918

5144

I decided to write about Evelyn's diary because it is an unusual find. It reveals the hope and the despair of dealing with the deadly disease of tuberculosis. Other sufferers have told their stories, but this diary is compelling because it was written by someone so young during hospitalization. Evelyn wrote every day, just as things were happening to her at the moment. She coped bravely by living her life as fully as she could under the circumstances of facing a devastating illness and the loss of many friends to the epidemic over time.

Tuberculosis, a contagious disease caused by bacteria that usually affected the lungs, was widespread during the time that Evelyn came down with it, but tuberculosis treatment was not the same then as it is today. Antibiotics had not been discovered. Rest and nursing care in a sanatorium, a hospital just for tuberculosis patients, was really the only available treatment. Since a diagnosis of tuberculosis often meant a death sentence, hospitalization with around-the-clock care in hope of bringing about a cure was desperately sought, but even that minimal treatment was not available to everyone. The disease kept spreading and many died who could not find or afford sanatorium care.

Curing in a sanatorium was a slow process. The word "cure" was really a misnomer because the disease was chronic and likely to flare up again. Many patients did get well, but sadly, many died. Sadly too, tuberculosis usually struck young adults like Evelyn, who was in her late teens, and others in their twenties and thirties. Long term confinement in an institution was not easy for anyone to accept, let alone an energetic sixteen-year-old girl. Curing from tuberculosis was not then a matter of taking the right medicine. It was a way of life that was not particularly normal for a teenager.

Evelyn's diary contains a fascinating account of what it was like to be ill with a very dangerous disease at such a young age. Yet, as with young people everywhere, there were good times at the Ray Brook State Hospital, and being with other young people from around the state who had the same disease may have helped her and others to cope. Evelyn had lots of friends at Ray Brook, including several boyfriends, who were also patients. They were all in the same boat. Patients, typically, did have "fond memories" of curing.

Evelyn poured out her most intimate feelings about her situation in her diary, but I feel sure she would forgive us for delving into her "secrets." I believe this because she later donated her Ray Brook diary to the nearby Saranac Lake Free Library in Saranac Lake, New York, where it has been preserved ever since. I discovered that Evelyn worked as an assistant to the librarian for a year or so after she left Ray Brook. As she grew older, she may have realized how interesting the diary might be to history lovers like me. I live in Saranac Lake. I have also worked at the library, more recently, and that is when I found the diary there.

Evelyn's diary has captivated people who are interested in tuberculosis curing in Saranac Lake. I also like the way it brings history alive through the telling of one very ordinary person's own experience. Evelyn is someone I can relate to and imagine what it would have been like living in the eventful year of 1918. This is the value of diaries, like Anne Frank's about the holocaust, and also one as interesting as Evelyn's about tuberculosis.

The diary ends abruptly before the end of 1918, which is startling because Evelyn wrote faithfully every day up until then. Of course, Evelyn had not been well and a feeling of dread comes over most readers when the writing stops suddenly. In fact, it has long been suspected that Evelyn's story, had it been completed in that diary, may have had an early tragic ending. No one has seemed to know anything beyond the diary itself about this young Evelyn Bellak who cured in the Adirondack Mountains so long ago. The 1930 United States Census revealed the fact that she worked at the library. I was intrigued and thought it would be fun to do more research and try to find out what really happened to Evelyn. Did she live a long life or die young? If she lived, was she able to have a normal life?

In thinking about writing a book, I also knew that teachers and students ask for information about Saranac Lake's famous history as a site for curing tuberculosis, where many patients did recover with proper care. The diary seemed to me a perfect focus for telling the tuberculosis story from a young patient's point of view. Discovering a treasure trove of photographs of Evelyn and her fellow patients at Ray Brook during my research was serendipitous. How lucky can a researcher get? I hope that both teens and adults will be interested in this book. I have added several sidebars with relevant historical background of the time period, and have defined terms that may be unfamiliar in the text.

Tuberculosis—Biographical & Historical Aspects

Evelyn Confronts Tuberculosis

For many, many years before the diary was written in 1918, there had been *epidemics* of tuberculosis, that is, times when the disease spread very rapidly. Tuberculosis was the leading cause of death in American cities crowded with large numbers of immigrants who were moving in at a rapid rate. Although tuberculosis was understood as contagious by that time, there was still no sure cure for the disease. An advanced case of tuberculosis was generally considered fatal. Public health officials in New York City inspected tenements and found tuberculosis bacteria in the rooms of the sick. The bacteria seemed to hide in dust. Almost everyone was exposed to tuberculosis, but most healthy people were able to fight it off.

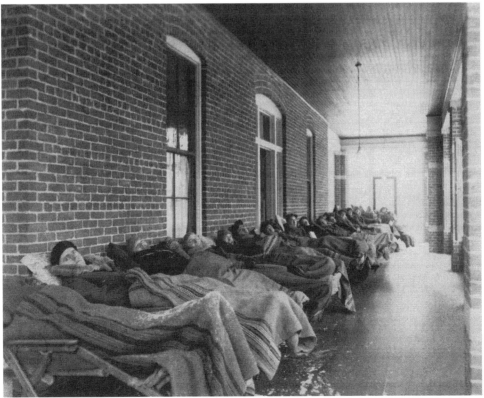

Curing patients. Courtesy of the Adirondack Collection, Saranac Lake Free Library 86.609K

The individuals who, for whatever reason, came down with the disease were likely to die of it, slowly, as the bacteria multiplied in the body. Although there were no drugs for tuberculosis, there were hospitals and sanatoriums[1], like Ray Brook Hospital, where patients could rest and be taken care of to try to build up their strength to fight the disease.

When we meet Evelyn through the diary, she is struggling with the disease and the first thing we know about her is that she has tuberculosis at age sixteen. How she handles her illness reveals her personality and her true character, and also gives us an idea of what it must have been like for the huge numbers of young adults who had tuberculosis at the time. Rest was all that could be offered as a possible cure, so that's what people tried to do because it was their only hope. Resting in a hospital or a sanatorium meant that you had someone watching over you, healthy meals prepared for you and a doctor's care when you needed it.

The "rest cure," as it was known, sometimes got people well enough to live a more normal life, but it was a very slow process. The idea of resting does not seem at all hard to do, but the diary shows that curing required a lot of patience. Lying on a recliner, outdoors in the fresh air ideally, and simply resting without moving around was pretty much the routine. It must have been a bit like having a cold today and being told to rest in order to get better (and there is not much else you can do for a cold, even now). With tuberculosis though, it usually took at least a year of rest, often several years. And unlike a cold, you weren't at all sure that you would get well from tuberculosis. Evelyn recorded the number of hours she "cured" on various days. For example, she wrote in her diary: *cured for three hours and a half this afternoon* (January 6).

As I began reading the diary, I quickly understood that Evelyn was only too well aware of the possibility of death. She corresponded with many former patients who had gone home, keeping in touch with old friends. She enjoyed receiving letters but, early in the diary, Evelyn wrote: *Mother got a letter from Mrs. Cawley...they've moved...Trilly died. Poor girl*! (January 9). Trilly may have been a former patient at Ray Brook, in any case, a young friend who had died. That same day Evelyn was examined by a doctor and was told she was "positive," meaning she had an active and contagious case of "TB," as tuberculosis was referred to, TB for *tubercle bacillus*, the bacterium that causes the disease. It is not known what her exact diagnosis had been upon admittance to the hospital. She stated that she had been "negative" when she came to Ray Brook about three months earlier, perhaps early October, 1917. Evelyn may not have understood the details of her diagnosis, but certainly knew that "positive" was not good.

Evelyn often felt discouraged during her stay at Ray Brook Hospital: *I'm just about sick and tired of the whole game...I don't believe I'll ever get one bit better than I am. I don't see the use of staying here.* (August 26). The daily regimen of curing was undoubtedly hard on a teenager who wanted to be active. *Same old routine, Diary...Get up, eat, cure, eat, cure, go to bed* (September 29). But Evelyn's diary shows that, fortunately, she was *ambulatory*, which meant that she was well enough to get out of bed and walk around at times. Not all patients had that much freedom.

Tuberculosis patients experienced coughing, night sweats, fever and weight loss. When patients became very sick, they even coughed up blood. Evelyn wrote about *coughing all the time* (May 27), but was reprimanded by the nurse about alarming new patients by purposely coughing as a joke. Evelyn showed her mischievous nature when she wrote: *Miss Cleland called us down for coughing at new patients. I don't believe she knows what a joke is* (August 9)[2]. It was no joke because tuberculosis germs are spread by coughing, but making a joke out of it probably helped the young people at the hospital to cope.

Evelyn's temperature was taken daily and recorded on a chart. She often recorded her temperature's ups and downs in her diary too, worrying whenever it went up. Maintaining her weight was also very important, another thing to worry about. *Gained ¼ lb., but had on heavier clothing so that I'm just about the same. If only I don't lose any more* (August 15). Before the identification of the tubercle bacillus by German physician Robert Koch in 1882, tuberculosis was called "consumption" because it slowly consumed its victims, making them gradually thinner and weaker.[3] Evelyn was quite thrilled when she occasionally gained weight, even just a little—a reason to hope.

Edward Livingston Trudeau, M.D. Courtesy of the Adirondack Collection, Saranac Lake Free Library P82.19

"Little Red" Cure Cottage. Courtesy of the Adirondack Collection, Saranac Lake Free Library P82.101

"Pioneer Health Resort"

As unlucky as Evelyn and her hospital mates were for having tuberculosis, they were lucky to be in an area of the country where tuberculosis was being studied and treatment was becoming a specialty. The nearby village of Saranac Lake, located in New York State's Adirondack Mountains, was a major center for research in and the treatment of tuberculosis until antibiotics came along, and was the reason Ray Brook State Hospital, subsidized by the State of New York, was located just a few miles away. Saranac Lake had long been described as a health resort because of its fresh mountain air. In 1869, William H.H. Murray published a book called *Adventures in the Adirondacks* in which he made it seem as though spending time outdoors in the Adirondack Mountains could cure just about anything. Murray's book was popular and opened up a flood of tourists from densely populated urban areas where a number of diseases, often deadly, could spread very fast. In a time when contagion was not as well understood as it is today and medical cures were primitive at best, people who could afford to travel were encouraged to spend leisure time in the outdoors, particularly in the fresh mountain air, to maintain good health.

Dr. Edward Livingston Trudeau, who graduated from medical school in 1871 and practiced medicine in New York City, was one of these health seeking visitors to the Adirondacks. Saranac Lake eventually became famous as a site for curing tuberculosis because of him. Dr. Trudeau loved hunting and fishing in the vast northern woods near the Canadian border. In 1873, when he was in his twenties, Dr. Trudeau came down with tuberculosis several years after his own brother had died of the disease. He was very aware that there was no cure for tuberculosis and he expected to die just as his brother had. Dr. Trudeau made the brave and grim decision to spend his last days in his beloved Adirondacks. Instead, he recovered and soon made Saranac Lake his home.

Trudeau began to encourage other TB sufferers to come for the wilderness rest cure. In 1884, he built "Little Red," a tiny "cure cottage" just large enough to accommodate two patients.[4] This was the beginning of his Adirondack Sanitarium which he enlarged building by building as it became the foremost treatment center for tuberculosis in the United States. Dr. Trudeau was a renowned leader in both treatment and research, building the first laboratory for tuberculosis research in the United States. Saranac Lake began to advertise itself as a health resort and tuberculosis care rapidly became a flourishing business, as independent cure cottages and sanatoriums were built throughout the Village of Saranac Lake. There were so many people arriving with the disease that it was difficult to accommodate all of them. Several large hospitals were also built in surrounding villages, including the Ray Brook State Hospital, which took in New York State residents who could not afford to pay for their care.

The Founding of the New York State Hospital
At Ray Brook

The New York State legislature appropriated funds for a state hospital for tuberculosis patients at the turn of the twentieth century.[5] Dr. Edward Baldwin from Saranac Lake, a co-worker with Dr. Trudeau, helped to select an appropriate site with mountain views within the State Forest Preserve. The chosen unspoiled site was located just four miles from Saranac Lake and on the road to Lake Placid, six miles further.

Ray Brook State Hospital for the Treatment of Tuberculosis, taken between 1905 and 1920. Courtesy of Library of Congress Digital Collections LC-D4-36949

The hospital building was opened in 1904, but before it was ready, patients cured in tents. Tents continued to be used during the summer months for decades after. Evelyn mentioned them in her diary: *It is beautiful by the tents. I'd love to go* (May 24). It must have been fun camping out except for the mosquitoes and black flies buzzing around. A new wing was added to the hospital building in 1911 that doubled its capacity to 300. Male and female patients were housed in separate dormitories.[6]

Tent curing at Ray Brook. Courtesy of the Adirondack Collection, Saranac Lake Free Library 83.583

Patients had to be legal residents of New York State for at least one year to receive the care offered at Ray Brook at no cost. The hospital was required to give preference to poor patients and admit paying patients only when there was room. Patients were also supposed to have *incipient* tuberculosis in order to be admitted. This meant early cases with mild symptoms, such as slight fever and slight cough, because the disease was considered treatable at that stage. But patients who traveled to Ray Brook from across New York State often had more advanced cases. Tuberculosis sufferers who were sent to Ray Brook because they could not afford the cost of a private sanatorium may have delayed seeking diagnosis and treatment. Application for admission was made through the Health Officer or the Poor Officer of the home county which paid transportation and a regular medical fee to the hospital. A medical examination of the patient was also forwarded to the hospital. State law required that every case of tuberculosis be registered with local boards of health.[7]

After patients were accepted, they traveled to Ray Brook which could be reached by the Adirondack Division of the New York Central Railroad or by the Delaware and Hudson Railroad. The hospital had its own railroad station nearby, just down a hill. In the diary, Evelyn did not mention her arrival, but repeatedly describes scenes of "seeing off" friends who were well enough to go home, often several at a time. Many photographs were taken of these happy events at the railroad station.

Patient send-off. Courtesy of Helen Ryan Garlock

Since tuberculosis was rampant in urban environments, a substantial number of patients at Ray Brook came from large cities around New York State, areas where a lot of immigrants lived. My analysis of the United States Census Records for 1920 indicates that 22% of the 297 patients then at Ray Brook were foreign born, and 47% had a parent, and usually both parents, who were foreign born. I discovered that Evelyn Bellak was one of those patients with an immigrant background.

Evelyn Bellak's Family History

Evelyn circled three dates on the calendar inside the front cover of her diary. I learned that these were family birthdays: hers, her mother's and her father's. Family was important to her. It is clear from the diary that Evelyn was Jewish. She wrote frequently about attending the Saturday services held at Ray Brook, sometimes led by a rabbi and sometimes by a Jewish patient.

I had started looking for Evelyn and her family on the internet and in census records. Once I determined where the family had lived, I was able to dig further into the vital records of states and municipalities, and the historical records of libraries. I learned that Evelyn was born on August 20, 1901 in York, Pennsylvania.[8] She was the only child of Fanny (Rothstein) and Adolph (spelled Adolf in earlier records) Bellak. According to the United States Census of 1900, Adolph, then a merchant at a shop in the City of York, was a Jewish immigrant born in Vienna, Austria in 1866. He immigrated to the United States in 1883, at about 17 years of age, and filed a petition in New York City to become a *naturalized* (U.S.) citizen in 1889. He was required to swear to renounce all allegiance to the Emperor of Austria in order to become a citizen. Adolph's brother, Jacob, also a resident of York, Pennsylvania, acted as his witness for the naturalization process.

The two brothers had obtained peddler's licenses in the City of York throughout the 1890s. Peddlers sold good from pushcarts and horse drawn carts in the streets and were required by Pennsylvania law to purchase licenses for a fee of about $25.00 per year, depending on whether you were on foot, had a one horse cart or a two horse cart. Laws like this were set up to prevent *vagrancy* (homelessness), a significant problem due to widespread poverty among the large numbers of newly arriving immigrants. A Peddler's license application required a medical certification of disability because the poor were normally required by law to do manual labor, such as road work, to provide for their own support. Otherwise, county governments were mandated by the state to care for the poor. Adolph and his brother Jacob were both considered disabled. Applicants also needed someone to swear to their good character and help post a bond of $300.00.[9] Adolph had two horses and a wagon and sold clothing, dry goods (fabrics), and notions (thread, buttons, etc.)[10] I wondered how successful peddling dry goods had been and found out from census records that he had profited enough to open a shop on South George Street in York.

Peddler, East Side, New York City, undated. Courtesy of Library of Congress Digital Collection LC-DIG-ggbain-22928

Apparently, Adolph had also earned enough income from peddling to support a wife. I learned from a newspaper archive that Jacob Bellak had travelled to Manhattan to be a witness at his brother Adolph's marriage by a rabbi to Fanny Rothstein on October 31, 1899. The couple spent their honeymoon at the Colonial Hotel in Philadelphia before settling in York.[11] I wonder how they met. Fanny Rothstein, Evelyn's mother, was born on December 18, 1869, in New York City, the daughter of Eva (Wald) and Joseph Rothstein.[12] So Fanny was not an immigrant herself, but the daughter of immigrants. According to census records, Eva Wald was born in Prussia (now Germany) and Joseph Rothstein was born in Russia. He was a tailor. But something happened to Fanny's father, Evelyn's grandfather, after the 1870 Census was taken. He either died or left because Fanny's mother remarried. Supporting a family in the face of widespread poverty was very difficult and the abandonment of families by fathers was a serious problem at that time. In 1880, according to the U.S. Census, Fanny was living with her mother and her step-father, Louis

Oschinsky, who was born in Poland. They lived on Norfolk Street on the Lower East Side of Manhattan.

Jewish Immigration to New York

History Sidebar

The Lower East Side was home to a large number of Jewish immigrants. There was a *synagogue*, a Jewish place of worship, on Norfolk Street near where Evelyn's mother Fanny lived as a child. The largest number of Jewish immigrants in the United States came from Eastern European countries, such as Russia, in the late 1880s and 1890s because of anti-Jewish sentiment and oppression in their homelands. The assassination in 1881 of Tsar Alexander II of Russia was blamed on the Jews. Other Jewish groups had come earlier to America, but many of the later immigrants came to the United States to escape Russian *pogroms*

Apartment sweat shop, Lewis Wickes Hines, 1911 Courtesy of Library of Congress Digital Collection LC-DIG-nclc-04105

(organized massacres) which attacked Jews. Most of these later Jewish immigrants settled in New York City, particularly the Lower East Side. Members of Evelyn's mother's family were German Jews, one of the earlier immigrant groups which tended to settle farther north in Manhattan. But Fanny's father was Russian and her stepfather was from Poland, and Fanny spent at least part of her childhood on the Lower East Side.

Immigrants landing at Castle Garden, wood engraving, A.D. Shults, 1880. Courtesy of Library of Congress Digital Collection LC-USZ 62-99403

Jews who immigrated to America believed they would be more welcome and would have a chance of becoming more prosperous there. Jewish (and other) immigrants from Europe would have had to save for a long time to get enough money to travel to America by ship. They could ride most cheaply in *steerage*, a part of the ship below decks that was very crowded and gave them an uncomfortably rough ride at sea. They looked forward to jobs, however, and planned to start a new life. Immigrant workers were very much needed because there were not enough American workers to fill the demand during the Industrial Revolution. Most of these jobs were in garment factories and *sweat shops* in cities like New York, where working conditions were not the best.

Passing the Inspecting Physician, wood engraving, 1866. Courtesy of Library of Congress Digital Collection LC-USZ62-37828

The pay was low for immigrant workers and the hours were long but factory jobs at least provided a steady income. Factory owners liked hiring immigrant workers because they were willing to work for lower pay than native born citizens. Women and children of immigrant families often worked as well, for very low wages, to supplement the family income, sometimes working in their homes doing *piece work* (work, such as sewing, done and paid for by the piece).

When the ships arrived from Europe carrying Evelyn's ancestors, the passengers may have been processed at Castle Garden in New York City. Castle Garden operated from 1855 to 1889 and was located in southern Manhattan, within walking distance of the Lower East Side. Ellis Island opened later because Castle Garden was not large enough to handle the growing number of immigrants. Millions of people were processed at Ellis

Island. Upon arrival, immigrants underwent questioning and a physical examination, then registration. Some were sent back as undesirables because of illness or for other reasons. Some were sent to be *quarantined* (kept isolated) for a period of time because of contagion.[13]

There was considerable *nativist* sentiment (protecting the interests of native inhabitants against those of immigrants) among the American people, particularly among Anglo-Saxon Protestants who were, of course, descendants of earlier immigrants from northern European countries. Nativists looked down on the newer immigrants who spoke strange languages, dressed differently and had unfamiliar religious practices. Nativists were hostile to Jews and Catholics because they believed that the *Nordic race* (made up of white Protestants) was superior. The United States Congress tried several times to pass laws requiring literacy tests for immigrants; these tests were obviously impossible for a foreign language speaker to pass. Several presidents vetoed the bills, but eventually a bill passed in 1917, over President Woodrow Wilson's veto. A quota system, established in 1921, limited the number of immigrants from various countries and a 1924 National Origins Quota Act limited immigrants to mostly those from British, German, and Scandinavian countries.[14] German Jews, like Evelyn's ancestors, had become more acceptable at that time because they had already *assimilated* (become Americanized). At this time, prejudice against Jewish immigrants from Southern and Eastern European countries was based more on class and economics than religion. *Anti-Semitism* (prejudice against Jews) only grew, however, before World War II.

Dense populations of Jewish immigrants lived in tenements that lined the streets of the Lower East Side. A *tenement* was an apartment building about 6 to 8 stories high. A lot of children were born and raised in tenements like those on Norfolk Street. Large families lived in just a few small, very crowded rooms, often sleeping shoulder to shoulder on make-shift beds. Bathroom facilities were scarce and had to be shared. Family life was very important to these Jewish immigrants, though, and neighbors often helped out needy neighbors. Because of widespread poverty, most people were on their own for medical care, though public health nurses might come around during epidemics. Quarantines were sometimes set up in the tenements to prevent the spread of disease. And Jews were often blamed, unfairly, for tuberculosis.[15] Life was pretty hard then.

Tenement House, New York City. Lewis Wickes Hine, 1910. Courtesy of Library of Congress
Digital Collection LC-DIG-nclc-04078

Tenement, Elizabeth Street, New York City, Lewis Wickes Hines, 1912. Courtesy of Library of Congress Digital Collection LC-DIG-nclc-04208

Tuberculosis Strikes Evelyn's Family

Evelyn Bellak was born on August 20, 1901 in York, Pennsylvania. Sometime before 1910, Adolph Bellak, Evelyn's father, contracted tuberculosis. His health apparently had been impaired for some time by an unidentified ailment (blotted out in peddler's license records for privacy reasons) which caused him a lot of pain. The United States Census of 1910 lists him as a patient at White Haven Sanatorium in White Haven, Luzerne County, Pennsylvania, at some distance from York where Evelyn, then age 8, and her mother Fanny were living alone at a boarding house. White Haven Sanatorium was founded as a free hospital for poor people suffering from tuberculosis at about the same time as the Ray Brook Hospital in New York State. It was located in farm country, away from the pollution of cities, but within easy reach by rail for patients from Philadelphia. Similar to Ray Brook, White Haven began with tents for curing patients.[16] By 1909, the sanatorium began charging for patient care. Unlike Ray Brook, all cases were accepted, regardless of the stage of the disease.

It is hard to imagine how the family managed financially in those days while Adolph was sick. At some point, Adolph recovered enough from tuberculosis to move his family north to Endicott, New York, in Broome County, near Binghamton. Evelyn mentioned Endicott in the diary: *nothing seen of any packages from Endicott as yet* (June 25). She was waiting for a dress to wear on the Fourth of July being sewn by someone named Helen, possibly a cousin. The New York State Census of 1915 indicates that Adolph, at age 47, had by then lived in the United States for 28 years.[17] He was the proprietor of a dry goods store in Endicott, while Fanny kept house and Evelyn attended school. Local newspapers begin listing Evelyn as an honor student in the seventh grade in 1914, continuing right through tenth grade in 1917. She was a Camp Fire Girl and is pictured as having been a member of the high school basketball team.[18] Endicott was a booming industrial center where all of the tanneries for the shoe industry that became Endicott Johnson were located. Living in Endicott would have been a very different experience for Evelyn than living in the colonial city of York.

Endicott Johnson Factory

History Sidebar

The Endicott Johnson factory was the largest shoe manufacturing operation in the world at the time the Bellak family lived in the Village of Endicott. Endicott's factory owners recruited Eastern European workers and, reportedly, immigrants frequently asked, "Which way EJ?" upon their arrival at Ellis Island.[19] By 1910, there were Austrian immigrants (like Adolph Bellak) as well as Hungarians, Russians and Italians living in Endicott. And some of these immigrants were Jewish. Adolph may have felt that he would be comfortable with and perhaps helpful to the newcomers. He himself had been a tanner when he first came to New York City.

George F. Johnson established the shoe manufacturing company after having grown up around and working in shoe factories in Massachusetts from the age of 13. With the financial help of Henry B. Endicott of Boston, Johnson carried out his vision of a model corporate community in which a factory would be surrounded by employee owned homes in the country side, away from the city.[20] Johnson chose a farmland site west of Binghamton. Various factory buildings in what became the villages of Johnson City and Endicott handled all aspects of the business from tanning the leather to boxing up the shoes and selling them.

Johnson created a program of "corporate welfare" in which the company took care of the medical needs, housing and social activities of employees. Johnson's wife opened her Ideal Training School in 1917 to teach immigrant women how to keep house and cook healthy "American meals," and she also set up a day nursery for children of women who worked in the factories. Native born workers were encouraged to help immigrant employees adjust to their new situation. And by 1920, one third of the workers were foreign born.[21]

Adolph must have thought about the possibility of numerous potential customers who received regular wages at the large factory. The population of Endicott surged from about 2,400 in 1910 to about 10,000 in 1917. Relocating to Endicott would have been a wise move for Adolph, and it was an interesting community.

Washington Street, Endicott, New York, with shoe factory in background. Adolph Bellak's store would have been down the street on the left, next to the hotel where he stayed. Courtesy of Broome County Historical Society

Adolph Bellak had arrived at Endicott in 1914, the year he was first listed in the City Directory, and boarded at the hotel until he got established. He soon brought Fanny and Evelyn there and, in 1915, the family lived in an apartment just across the street from the large shoe factory. Adolph had saved enough money to open his own dry goods store on Washington Avenue, right next to the hotel, undoubtedly, planning for a more normal life for his family. And it was surely a prosperous life he sought. In fact, many successful businesses established in those days have been passed down to family members who still own them today. But, since his tuberculosis recurred and Evelyn was also afflicted, this hoped for life would not be possible for the Bellak family.

Whether Evelyn was infected with tuberculosis from contact with her father or she picked it up in Endicott cannot be known. There were over 500 cases of tuberculosis in Broome County during 1916, most in the city of Binghamton, but the crowded working conditions in the rural factories also spread disease. In fact, tuberculosis was more common in shoe factories than all other manufacturing combined, according to a 1918 industrial report.[22] There was concern about the lack of light and ventilation in factory workrooms. Workers were often tired and experienced stress from "speed ups" in their work rate, being paid for doing piece work rather than by the hour.

Whatever the source, Evelyn contracted tuberculosis and was sent, at the age of 16, to the State Hospital at Ray Brook, where she could receive care at the expense of the State of New York. Evelyn indicates in her diary that her mother had been in the employ of the Ray Brook Hospital since late September or early October of 1917, so that must have been the approximate date of Evelyn's admission. Fanny went along and lived on the grounds at Ray Brook to be near her daughter. Surely, she didn't want her young daughter and only child to be ill and far away. Fanny worked as a waitress at the hospital. By working at Ray Brook, she could look after Evelyn and also earn a little income; she would soon be the only family member well enough to do so. Adolph did not go with them to Ray Brook, but continued to work out of Endicott. Although the family was separated again, at least Adolph was employed at the time. His occupation was described as "commercial traveler" in 1917. He may have worked for Endicott Johnson or continued to sell dry goods on the road for a while.

Adolph eventually "broke down" again with tuberculosis and, at some point, was hospitalized nearby at what became the Broome County Tuberculosis Hospital at Chenango, New York. This facility was built in 1919, replacing the very small Mountain Sanatorium which only had 17 beds and did not admit young people of Evelyn's age. Adolph was no longer living in Endicott by 1918 and Evelyn's diary indicates that he was ill at that time so he may have been at the Mountain Sanatorium. In 1919, the rate at Broome County was $10.00 a week, according to ability to pay, but the *Directory of Sanatoria Hospitals and Day Camps for the Treatment of Tuberculosis in the United States* indicates that those unable to pay received free treatment. Why Adolph did not go to Ray Brook is a bit of a mystery, but at that point there was a county hospital for adults and the county may not have wanted to pay for his transportation to Ray Brook, as they were obligated to do for Evelyn because of her age. This was a very sad situation for the family.

Evelyn's Ray Brook Diary

Evelyn and Fanny at Ray Brook

Obviously, Ray Brook Hospital did accept 16 year olds when Evelyn was admitted. There is no record of the written policy for 1917, but children were admitted in 1908 and in later periods. The United States Census of 1920 includes one 11 year old and two 15 year old patients at Ray Brook.

Evelyn felt guilty about her mother having to work at the hospital and worried about her health. She wrote about a bad fall Fanny had in the dining room that landed her in bed for two days (January 21). Another diary entry in May indicated that her mother was not well, and Evelyn felt responsible. *Oh, I am worried about her,* she wrote, *If anything should be wrong with her, I never could forgive myself* (May 9). After suffering through an awful cold, Fanny was granted a week's vacation to rest. Evelyn believed that her mother was certainly entitled to a rest, *having been in the employ of the State for a year* (October 3). Of course, Fanny worried about Evelyn too. When Evelyn's temperature rose to 100 degrees, her nurse reported it to Fanny: *Mrs. V told Mother and she worries of course* (January 20). And they both worried about Dad. *Mother got a letter from Dad. He seems sort of down hearted. Poor fellow! I suppose he's awfully lonely* (January 7). Of course, there were mother-daughter arguments too. She would occasionally write: *Mother and I had a scrap* (January 13). They argued over Evelyn's behavior with some boyfriend, or perhaps her not resting enough.

A departure. Courtesy of Helen Ryan Garlock

Evelyn ardently hoped to get better quickly and return home to Endicott, but she really had no idea how long she would have to spend curing. She must have known the length of stay at Ray Brook varied from a few months to several years, but she hoped it would only be a year in her case. Evelyn chronicled many of the comings and goings of the friends made during her cure at Ray Brook. Some patients were well enough to go home for short visits. Some patients found it necessary to leave for personal reasons, such as a family emergency. Some patients got well and left, only to return, sick again, soon after.

Girls of the East Wing - Apr. 1918

Helen Ryan, second row, second from left. Evelyn Bellak second down from small left rear pillar by staircase. Courtesy of Helen Ryan Garlock

Helen Ryan, an Irish Girl

A person in the next bed at Ray Brook might have been any one of all sorts of nationalities and religions. But that was less significant than the bond of curing the patients shared. Of course, Evelyn knew many Jewish patients, but one of the best of Evelyn's many friends at Ray Brook was Helen Ryan, an Irish girl. Helen and Evelyn both roomed in the women's East Wing of the Hospital. Helen is very important to this story because she put together the photograph album that supplied many of the photographs of Ray Brook patients in this book.

Helen Ryan's Album. Author Photograph

Evelyn often wrote: *walked with Helen.* On January 26: *went out walking with Helen and Pauline Nold. Took pictures on the road.* Helen must have taken the following picture of Evelyn and Pauline that very day, and Pauline the picture of Evelyn and Helen. I learned about Helen's photographs at the Saranac Lake Free Library while I was researching the diary. Helen's niece and namesake,

Helen Ryan Garlock, had given copies of many Ray Brook photographs to the library without even realizing that Evelyn's diary was there. A student doing

Taking pictures at 37° below

Evelyn and Pauline

research at the library realized the connection between the two documents. I contacted Mrs. Garlock and she told me about Helen, showed me the original album, and shared more family photographs. And much to my delight, Evelyn was identified in a few of the album's photographs. And an amazing thing is that she turned out to be the one I had picked out in the photocopies at the library as possibly Evelyn!

Helen's story is particularly poignant because, though she made the most of her time at Ray Brook, making new friends and joining in activities, her tuberculosis was not cured there. Helen was born in 1897 so she was about four years older than Evelyn. She was the seventh child of Patrick and Ellen Ryan of Norway, in Herkimer County, New York. Patrick Ryan was born in 1855 in Canada where his parents had emigrated from Ireland. He became a United States citizen in 1885 and owned a dairy farm in Herkimer County where his children were born.

Ryan Family. Helen is the young girl at center. Courtesy of Helen Ryan Garlock

Helen Ryan in nurse's uniform.
Courtesy of Helen Ryan Garlock

Helen Ryan was obviously a very beloved family member. Mrs. Garlock remembers Helen being described as somewhat of "a devil [who] loved to ride her horse and was very pretty." She had begun nurses training at Faxton Hospital in the City of Utica, New York, where she contracted tuberculosis. Sadly, this was a common occurrence for nurses and physicians who were training to care for the sick and often exposing themselves to infection. Helen's older sister Florence, born in 1892, taught school for a year, but hated it, then attended the Albany School of Pharmacy, graduating in 1915. She also contracted tuberculosis and both girls wound up at Ray Brook, as did their cousin Robert Murphy. Florence was mentioned in Evelyn's diary beginning in the fall of 1918. Her nickname was "Skip" and she did get well at Ray Brook. Cousin Bob did too and he became a Catholic priest. The family refers to him as "Father Bob."

Irish Immigrants

History Sidebar

A massive immigration from Ireland in the early 1800s helped to meet the need for laborers in American industry, such as large textile mills. Many arrived at Canadian ports, as well as Boston and New York. Canada was a British Province and that made it cheaper for Irish immigrants to board ships headed for Canada. It was not difficult to enter the United States from there and travel to New England mill towns. Some of the Irish stayed in Canada and some others migrated to the northern parts of Border States like New York and Vermont. Irish immigrants, similarly to other ethnic groups living in American cities, were confronted with tuberculosis and other contagious diseases linked to poverty and overcrowding.

Immigrants escaping poverty and famine due to crop failures in Ireland were more willing to work for lower wages than American workers. It seems to have been somewhat easier for Irish women to find decent jobs than for Irish men, and large numbers of Irish-born women worked. They often found jobs as domestic servants, cleaning, cooking, sewing and caring for children in middle-class homes. Most native-born American women considered domestic service degrading. But young Irish women were happy to be able to gain their economic independence and were also helped to begin a process of *acculturation*, or Americanization, while living and working in the middle-class homes.[23]

There was continuing prejudice against Eastern Europeans. And native-born Protestants feared that the Irish, rapidly "breeding" Catholic children, might take over city politics and Catholicism might become the dominant faith. Newly-arrived Irish immigrants were ridiculed as ignorant and ill-mannered, and the men in particular, as violent drunkards. Along with "Help Wanted" signs, "No Irish Need Apply" signs were posted.[24] But, like German Jews, large numbers of Irish immigrants who had arrived earlier because of the potato famines in Ireland during the early 1800s had already become Americanized by the time the throngs of Eastern European immigrants began to arrive. Although anti-Catholic sentiment grew with the increase in Catholic immigrants from Italy and the Slavic countries in U.S. cities, many Irish had, by then, become settled and successful. But the Ku Klux Klan, started in 1915, targeted these immigrant groups in addition to Blacks, setting fire to synagogues and Catholic churches around the country.

Helen Ryan probably had a pretty normal American upbringing at the family farm in rural New York State. And she joined the ranks of the first American-born generation of young Irish women who entered the profession of nursing. This was still the era of the "New Woman," a time when large numbers of young American women began working in professional fields previously limited to men. Others became teachers, and between 1900 and 1910, the largest ethnic group among New York City school teachers was comprised of daughters of Irish parents. Helen's sister Florence left teaching for what was probably an even better paying and more prestigious profession: pharmacy. The more recent arrivals of Italians and other Eastern Europeans actually boosted the status of the Irish by accepting the worst paid occupations at the time.[25]

Helen Ryan, second from left. Courtesy of Helen Ryan Garlock

A group of patients. Courtesy of Helen Ryan Garlock

The "Fun" Part of Curing at Ray Brook

Helen Ryan, second from right. Courtesy of Helen Ryan Garlock

In spite of their illness, Evelyn, Helen and the other patients became good friends and did a lot of things together just for fun. The girls' residence at Ray Brook was probably not unlike a school dormitory. Curing really was a good way to meet a lot of other young people and they were all more or less in the same boat, trying to get well and keep their spirits up. Helen Ryan is mentioned over and over throughout the diary, going for walks with Evelyn and the other girls, attending events, and posing for picture taking. Some patients who had cameras would have prints made for everyone. Evelyn commented in her diary on how good (or awful) the pictures were. Patients tried to cheer up each other and hospital routines were made as pleasant as possible. Dinner was always an occasion for which everyone dressed up. And there were card games after dinner.

The girls kidded around a lot. Evelyn and Miss Mac Lean (probably a nurse) played a trick on Helen, filling her room with a lot of things *too funny for words* (January 28). Then, Evelyn and Helen sprinkled another girl's powder all over her room. This time though, as Evelyn wrote, *She told Mother and I got the deuce* (January 30). Then someone played a trick on Evelyn: *everything imaginable was in my room* (March 1). The girls tricked the nurses too. Once they helped hide from the nurse a girl who didn't feel like going to cure in the tents.

Of course, there was no television in those days. Ray Brook patients did not even have radio until 1924. But they did have a Victrola (record player) and films. Popular movies were shown regularly for patients, and Evelyn was allowed to attend additional movies shown for employees with her mother. She mentioned

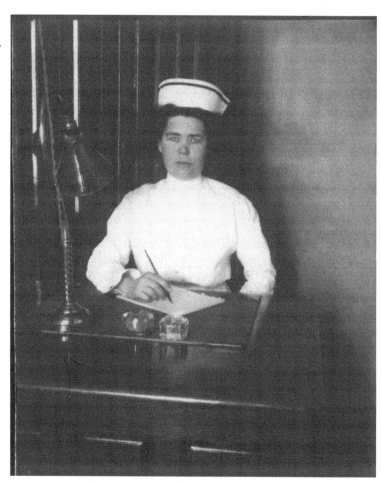

Unidentified Ray Brook nurse. Courtesy of the Adirondack Collection, Saranac Lake Free Library 86.584K

needing a permission slip to go to movies (January 15), presumably for medical reasons, or perhaps because of her age. The evening movies must have been a nice diversion and particularly enjoyable when the weather outside was bad, though patients were allowed to go out, even on cold days. During the winter there were horse-drawn sleigh rides, bobsled races for the boys, and occasionally a ride in an automobile. Evelyn had a date for a sleigh ride with a boy who had gallantly asked her mother's permission to invite her. On February 14, a group of patients rode all the way to Bloomingdale on snow covered roads (10 or so miles each way), so the sleigh rides were sometimes fairly long trips. Tuberculosis patients had to learn to embrace the Adirondack winters because they were required to cure outdoors at all temperatures. If you can believe Helen's album caption below the photograph on page 34, Evelyn and the girls apparently took walks on the hospital grounds, even when the temperature was thirty below zero!

SLEIGH RIDE to BLOOMINGDALE
32 MILES – FEB. 1918

Courtesy of Helen Ryan Garlock

On January 19, Evelyn went on a special outing with Helen and two other girls to Saranac Lake on *the 10:58* train for *shopping...and to the Berkeley for dinner*. Evelyn had sirloin steak, French fires, tomato salad, bread and butter, candy and hot chocolate. There was no need to watch her weight...on the contrary! The patients all tried hard to gain weight because tuberculosis made them too thin. After the dinner in Saranac Lake, the girls went to a movie in the village and then rode home in a sleigh. That wonderful meal must have spoiled Evelyn because the next night she wrote in her diary that she absolutely hated the dinners at the hospital.

In March, a group of patients put on a *minstrel show* (theatrical entertainment) for the whole hospital. Evelyn was not one of the entertainers but Helen was. She can be seen in the photograph dressed as Lady Liberty in her crown. Sometimes the East Wing put on some entertainment and invited the boys (Evelyn referred to patients as "girls" or "boys.") who stayed in the West Wing or the Pryor building. In the spring, there was a boat ride for everyone. On Decoration Day (now called Memorial Day), Evelyn attended a baseball game

Courtesy of Helen Ryan Garlock

between Pryor and the West Wing. There was another baseball game for the boys at the Fourth of July field day.

During very hot July weather, some of the girls wanted to go swimming after dinner though, apparently, it was not allowed. *Miss Levins was on duty* but she *looked the other way* and they were able to sneak out. Evelyn said they *had a great old time, till the boys came and watched us* (July 25). This was the second time in a week, though Evelyn corrected herself and called it *bathing*, not swimming. *I was afraid to swim on account of my old TB* (July 23.) There was another field day and ball game in September. Evelyn's favorite team (one of the boys' dorms) won: *Pryor won—2-1. Hooray!* (September 11). Dinner was served on the field that day, a picnic for a change.

Evelyn Bellak, left. Courtesy of Helen Ryan Garlock

A Halloween party was a big event for Evelyn. She wrote: *HALLOW-EEN...wonderful time...impromptu Halloween party and the boys came over. We played all sorts of games, and most of the girls dressed in gingham aprons with their hair down* (October 31). On November 12, Evelyn began rehearsing

43

for the *Thanksgiving stunt*. Helen Ryan was also in the show, or the "stunt," as Evelyn called it. It was a play about a school setting called *School Days. I'm to be Mary Jane & Helen Ryan Tige*, (November 12) she wrote. All of these activities helped a lot to take the patients' minds off their illness and provide some fun.

Silent Films

History Sidebar

The movies shown at Ray Brook in 1918 were silent films. Synchronous sound recording was not introduced in films until 1929. Some dialog was written out on the screen in separate film clips, interrupting the action, not like subtitles which are projected at the bottom of the screen in modern foreign language films. Actors would exaggerate their facial expressions and body language to help the audience understand the plot. Large theaters had organs and sometimes orchestras that played background music to provide emotional clues and special effects to go along with and enhance the story.[26]

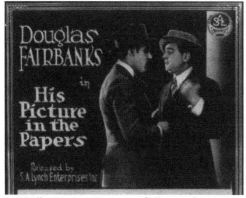

1918 Film Poster. Courtesy of Library of Congress Digital Collection LC-USZ62-83666

Most silent films were fairly short. Evelyn recorded the names of about seventy-five films and documentaries that she viewed within the ten and a half months she kept her diary. They were all current or recent films, ranging in dates from 1916-1918. Evelyn often mentioned the stars of the films she saw. Some famous ones were Douglas Fairbanks, Mary Pickford, Ethel Barrymore and Tom Mix. Cecil B. De Mille was a famous director of silent films. Since World War I was being waged at the time, some of the films shown at Ray Brook were war-related, but most were just for fun.[27]

Ray Brook Helps in the War Effort

The year of Evelyn's diary, 1918, turns out to have been a very interesting year in world history. The World War (now called World War I) had been going on all the while Evelyn was at Ray Brook and the patients were involved in the war effort. There was a large scale mobilization at home to support the troops.

World War I

History Sidebar

War broke out in Europe in 1914 after Archduke Franz Ferdinand of Austria was assassinated. Germany, Turkey and Austria-Hungary sided against England, France and Russia. Britain imposed a naval blockade of Germany, but German U-boats (submarines) began to attack ships. One ship, the *Lusitania*, was torpedoed and sunk in 1915 and over 100 Americans were killed. The United States entered the European war with Germany in April of 1917 even though American citizens were generally against participation. Immigrant Americans were divided because of loyalties to their homelands. But once war was declared over the continued threat of U-boat attacks, a wave of patriotism swept the country and 2.8 million men were inducted into military service, 2 million of them serving in Europe. The first American soldiers arrived in France in June, 1917. Allied forces succeeded in driving back the Germans in September of 1918, and by October, Germany had asked for an *armistice* (peace agreement). The armistice was negotiated and signed, ending the war on November 11, the day we now celebrate as Veterans' Day.

Women across the country helped in the war effort by doing volunteer work such as selling Liberty Bonds, which raised 23 billion dollars. In New York State each town had a *quota*, an amount of money to be raised in Liberty Bonds. A local newspaper published near Ray Brook, the *Lake Placid News*, urged local women to participate. "Every Woman and Girl Urged To Devote Spare Time In The Cause Most Vital To American Soldiers In This War" (February 8). An American Red Cross Chapter was formed in Saranac Lake to organize women volunteers who raised funds, did civilian relief work, produced supplies, packed and shipped them out, and provided education about the war effort.[28]

Red Cross women in Saranac Lake. Courtesy of the Adirondack Collection, Saranac Lake Free Library 83.18

The girls at Ray Brook, including Evelyn, volunteered to help the Red Cross. She mentioned knitting a Red Cross sweater in January. She soon finished it and began right away to knit another one. She *knitted and knitted till blue in the face* (January 17) because there was a deadline to meet. The Red Cross collected "odds and ends" of yarn from local residents that volunteers knitted into warm sweaters and socks for soldiers and refugees. The result was that the Saranac Lake Chapter of the Red Cross sent out 4,299 knitted garments over a 2-year period from April 1917 to April 1919. In May, Evelyn attended a Red Cross meeting where she made a sling for injured soldiers. The *Lake Placid News* article stated that the slings and surgical dressings made from donated sheets meant "life and death to our men" serving in the war. In those days, the government did not pay for everything needed by soldiers. Ordinary people all across the country donated goods and conserved food at home so there would be enough supplies for the troops.

Evelyn and Helen also helped with Red Cross fund raising. Patients from both Ray Brook and the Trudeau Sanatorium in Saranac Lake were asked to participate in a Red Cross Donation Day parade in Saranac Lake in April to boost Liberty Bond sales. Evelyn was excited: *They are going to have a parade over in Saranac Saturday for Bond Day. They want 24 girls from here to be in it...We're to be dressed as Red Cross nurses* (April 4). A special train was arranged to take them to Saranac Lake and some of the boys went too. Helen wore her Lady Liberty crown again for this event and led the Ray Brook group. Afterward, Evelyn wrote: *We girls from Ray Brook were without kidding the best part of the parade* (April 6).

Parade Day, Helen Ryan in Crown. Courtesy of Helen Ryan Garlock

Marching Unit. Helen Ryan in crown. Courtesy of the Adirondack Collection, Saranac Lake Free Library

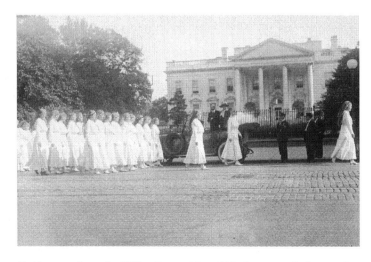

Similar parade at the White House, May 1918. Courtesy of Library of Congress Digital Collection LC-DIG-npcc-28116

Liberty Bond Day Parade. Courtesy of the Adirondack Collection of the Saranac Lake Free Library 05.13

Red Cross parade float, Washington, D.C. Harris & Ewing, 1917.
Courtesy of Library of Congress Digital Collection LC-DIG-hec-10875

Patients marching in the Liberty Bond Day parade. Courtesy of the Adirondack Collection of the Saranac Lake Free Library 05.12

Evelyn heard a Liberty Loan speaker and also mentioned in her diary having a War Saving Stamp. War Saving Stamps were sold cheaply, often to school age children, for 10 or 25 cents, and in this case, to patients who had little or no income. The stamps earned a small amount of interest and, when accumulated, could be redeemed for Liberty Bonds. Obviously, the patients tried to be informed and helpful in any way they could. In April, Evelyn's diary mentioned a raffle of Liberty Bonds held on one of the patients' movie nights. Also to raise funds, there was *dancing...[on] Wed. at the Red Cross jigger* (May 12).[29] Evelyn was very worried that she wouldn't know how to dance, something she was not used to doing.

Also in May, a ceremony was held for the raising of the *service flag*. A service flag was displayed at homes of families with a member in the military service. Villages, such as Lake Placid and Saranac Lake, displayed service flags containing a number of stars representing the number of men from the area who had enlisted. The soldiers represented by the flag at Ray Brook were probably staff members and/or former patients. Some of the physicians at Trudeau Sanatorium did Army service during the war.[30]

Evelyn attended a public Peace Mass held at Ray Brook Hospital on June 29. And there were lectures and a few movies about the war, including one entitled, *The Kaiser, Beast of Berlin*. (Kaiser Wilhelm II was the emperor of Germany.) In September, when the war was really raging in Europe, a touring Protestant minister gave a lecture on life in the trenches, having just returned from France. Evelyn wrote: *glad that I'm not over there as it isn't anything easy* (September 15).

It was a joyous occasion when news of the war's end came to the patients on November 7. Evelyn wrote: *PEACE* in her diary. It was announced in the dining room *that the Armistice with Germany had been signed. What a celebration we did have!* The patients marched to Pryor right then, and there was another parade at supper. *The West Wing fellows hung the Kaiser*, and there were *tableaux* (costumed people representing a scene) and other activities in MacDonald Solarium after supper (November 7).

Courtesy of Library of Congress Digital Collection
LC-USZC4-9559

Actually, the signing of the armistice occurred on the 11th, not the 7th, as Evelyn first wrote in the diary. Unknown to the patients at Ray Brook, a press release had been issued prematurely, in error. On November 11, Evelyn wrote in her diary: *Peace declared again for a change.* After noticing, while they were curing, a steady stream of cars heading toward Lake Placid, Evelyn, Helen and several other girls impulsively hired a car to go to Lake Placid for that village's victory parade. Evelyn said she had *more darn fun.* There was a similar parade in Saranac Lake and probably just about everywhere across the country. Trudeau Sanatorium patients marched in both local parades, in a unit headed by a hearse carrying an effigy of the Kaiser. Houses in Saranac Lake were decorated with flags and bunting, as they were across the nation, in celebration.

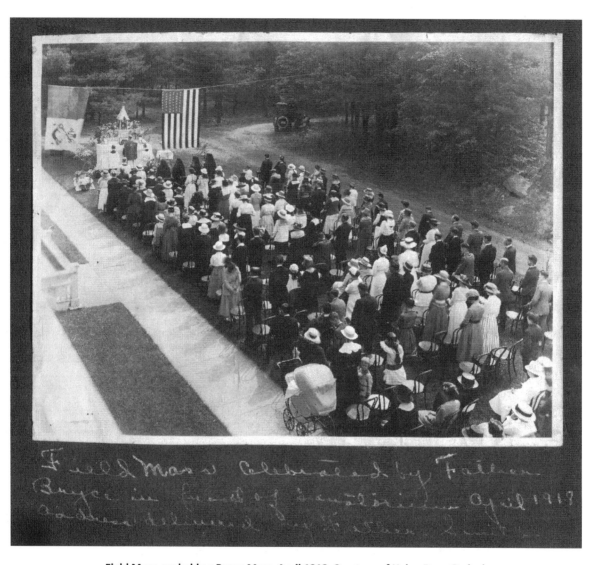

Field Mass, probably a Peace Mass, April 1918. Courtesy of Helen Ryan Garlock

Celebrating the Signing
of the Armistice.
Nov 11, 1918

Courtesy of Helen Ryan Garlock

End of war celebration, New York City. W.I. Drummond, 1918. Courtesy
of Library of Congress Digital Collection LC-DIG-ppmsca-09634

Another Red Cross Fundraiser. Courtesy of Helen Ryan Garlock

Time for Romance

Young males and females living in such close quarters, isolated from the rest of the world, and with time on their hands, were naturally quite interested in forming relationships with the opposite sex. When Evelyn began her diary with the words: *you must keep my secrets*, she may have meant her romantic thoughts. On January 2, she mentioned the first of several "boyfriends" she had during 1918. Evelyn wrote: *I'm dying for a letter from Jack*. It is apparent that she corresponded with Jack, a former patient, from January through October of that year. At first, she thought Jack might be coming back to Ray Brook, but learned that his health had improved and he would get a job. He may have missed Evelyn a lot because, after one of his letters, she wrote: *my darling Jack. Poor fellow he's so down-hearted* (February 28). He sent her his picture, and she wrote: *makes me sort of want to see him* (September 23).

But Evelyn was obviously not pining for Jack. There were too many interesting guys right there at Ray Brook. She often wrote about someone named Harry who liked her and apparently won out after a challenge from someone named Frank. Frank's name was dropped after this diary entry: *I'm in the awful fix. Both Frank and Harry are at me* (February 10). Soon after that, Evelyn said that at dinner she *put a make believe kiss on Harry's napkin but he didn't find it* (February 23). The girls did share some of their secrets with each other. Evelyn wrote a note to Harry...*something PRIVATE. However Sade & Peg know about it* (February 25). She wrote in her diary that she got Harry's ring and was wearing it, but added: *He doesn't care tho* (March 16). Whatever that meant, Harry soon left Ray Brook. Evelyn said she was glad...*rather tired of him*. And she quickly added: *There is a real cute little new fellow I'd like to get* (April 7).

She was soon introduced to the new fellow, Charles, who gave her a box of candy and made a date with her. She was *crazy about him* (April 14). She liked him *better than any of the fellows I've gone with, even Jack* (April 17). Yes, poor fellow, Jack! Evelyn and Charles argued a lot, though. Before long, she said she *almost broke up* with Charles (May 18), and finally, the relationship was doomed when another new guy arrived at Ray Brook. Charles was furious. He *was raving*, she wrote, about her relationship with the new guy. *I'll have to give him the grand bounce*, she decided, with rather a nasty tone (June 6). There was *sort of a scrap* between the two guys and both of them invited Evelyn on an upcoming boat ride. She was forced to choose and sent Charles a note saying that she was not going with him. At the back of the diary on a "Memoranda" page, Evelyn copied a poem about the incident written by Miss Mac Lean (her nurse):

Boat ride to Upper Saranac. Courtesy of Helen Ryan Garlock

> *Now Charlie on Evelyn did dote*
> *And invited her out on a boat*
> > *But pity his fix,*
> > *For Evelyn said, "Nix."*
> *In a cute little note that she wrote.*
>
> *Said she, "You have angered me so,*
> *That no longer can you be my beau,*
> > *No more you'll be sittin'*
> > *A holdin' my mitten⋯*
> *And by heck; it's with Jacobs I'll go.*

Courtesy of Helen Ryan Garlock

The new guy, named Morris Jacobs, had something in common with Evelyn. They saw each other at the Jewish services which were held on Saturdays, right at the hospital. Evelyn must have been a pretty good piano player because she played for the choir, in rehearsals and services. *Practiced hymns for Day of Atonement* (September 13). Her family may have owned a piano if she had learned to play so well. Owning a piano in those days was considered a status symbol, an indicator of a family's success. Choir rehearsals often drove Evelyn crazy because the boys fooled around and sounded terrible (*punk* was her word) and she threatened to quit, but didn't, at least not until October. Morris was elected to lead the services after the previous leader went home from the hospital. Sometimes Rabbi Lubin came down to Ray Brook from nearby Plattsburgh. Evelyn attended services faithfully but wrote: *I only hope he comes some night when there aren't any movies* (October 13).

Evelyn was really smitten this time. Morris's name was written on practically every page through the end of the diary. He was always very attentive and took her to Saranac Lake for her birthday. *Had one 'grand ridiculous' time today. Went over to Saranac on the 1:25...went to the Pontiac [Theater]. Afterwards we walked to the Lakewood Inn for supper: Steak!!! Rode from the Inn to the station in a car. More darn fun! Gee, I do like my little Morris tonight* (August 17). The next day she suffered some bad effects with her health, but said it was worth it. It wasn't long before she wrote: *Oh, Diary, I got my first kiss tonight* (September 2). Then, *Oh, Diary, I think I love him. That's no joke. I mean it* (October 29). At the Halloween party, *He tried to kiss me. I didn't let him tho. He must like me a little, mustn't he?* (October 31).

Often, the romances at sanatoriums were short-lived because patients came and left so frequently. Romantic relationships between patients were often referred to as "cousining" in Saranac Lake because of some patients' known commitments at home. Lonely patients tried to explain their romantic friends by referring to them as cousins. When Evelyn first wrote about Charles, she said he was *almost engaged* (April 17). Fanny Bellak must have watched Evelyn very closely to protect her from the married men at Ray Brook.

Both Courtesy of Helen Ryan Garlock

Unidentified Ray Brook Nurse. Courtesy of the Adirondack Collection, Saranac Lake Free Library 86.588K

The Rest Cure Regimen

It seems hard to believe that Evelyn was supposed to be curing from tuberculosis during all this busyness. Keep in mind, though that all of the reported activity in Evelyn's diary occurred over a period of 10½ months. Her diary, understandably, focused a bit more on social activities than on curing. Curing was boring. But in addition to jotting down her temperature and weight in the diary, Evelyn reported curing on most days, and occasionally how many hours she spent on the rest cure. For example, *Cured 4 hours today* (January 10) and *cured and cured and cured after supper* (April 29). Apparently, she was pretty much in charge of the number of hours, but had to submit requests in advance to "take a half day" or occasionally a full day off. She rarely mentioned being reminded to cure. And she was pretty persistent, even when it rained all day: *I stayed in the open with Sade's umbrella, so I didn't get wet* (May 7). And when activities interfered, she had to spend extra time on the cure: *cured a lot all day...to make up for yesterday* (May 31). When things were quiet, it was easier: *Cured a lot. Had to as there wasn't anything else to do* (September 10). She sometimes napped while curing: *It was so noisy on the cure, I thot I'd never get to sleep but I did—finally* (October 16). Obviously, not everyone napped.

Evelyn did occasionally report being told to lie outside in her cure chair: *Was chased out this morning, so cured a little. Cured real well this afternoon* (February 7), though she did not have a strict routine. When the Ray Brook patients settled down to cure, they sat out on comfortable "cure chairs" on large open porches. Cure chairs were typically sturdy wooden chaises on which you could put your feet

Courtesy of Helen Ryan Garlock

up and the back could be raised or lowered for comfort. These chairs had metal springs and a thick cushion, or mattress. They were standard equipment, manufactured in Saranac Lake and shipped to sanatoriums everywhere for use on enclosed porches. The cure chairs in Helen's photographs appear less sturdy and seem to be portable for taking out in the open air.

Because curing was a year-round activity, patients had to be protected from

Winter curing at Ray Brook Courtesy of the Adirondack Collection, Saranac Lake Free Library 86.610K

severe cold. Every patient at Ray Brook was assigned warm clothing consisting of long underwear, sweaters, long coats, mittens and wool hats. Additionally, layers of newspaper, up to six inches thick, were placed under the mattress for insulation. Patients also had "stone pigs" at their feet for warmth. Stone pigs were flattened crockery jugs filled with hot water and placed on their sides under the blankets. They were shaped a little like a fat pig with a snout.

Evelyn got books to read from the library and wrote many, many letters to family and friends. She wrote in the diary about knitting and crocheting while curing, not just for the war effort. Morris bought yarn for her to make him a sweater and she also knitted one for her Dad. The tuberculosis doctors in Saranac Lake, such as E.L. Trudeau, disapproved of too much activity for very sick patients, and fever was supposed to be a pretty clear indication of overdoing it. Rest meant rest—period. But recovering patients, when they were well enough, needed to learn

Stone pig. Author photograph

how to reenter society and find employment without wearing themselves down and becoming sick again.

Noted tuberculosis physician Dr. Lawrason Brown of Saranac Lake published a booklet, *Rules for Recovery From Tuberculosis*, in 1916, that was reprinted several times in later years. Dr. Brown's rules were strict about the necessary discipline of a medical recovery, but he also believed that recovering patients needed some preparation for returning to a normal life. He thought that *rehabilitation* ought to include some form of work along with lessons on how to maintain a healthy lifestyle in order to stay well. Because she sometimes worked too hard on her knitting, Evelyn might have benefitted from reading Dr. Brown's *Rules* : "Sewing, knitting or crocheting **for pleasure** or to pass the time are permitted, but those who feel they must finish so much every day should avoid them." "But," Dr. Brown recognized, "engaging in craft work helped fill the otherwise boring hours of rest" and a variety of crafts were taught in sanatoriums.[31]

From *Woodland Whispers* December, 1925

The Director of Ray Brook State Hospital, Dr. Harry A. Bray, also believed in recreation and rehabilitation. Dr. Bray began as an assistant physician at Ray Brook in 1907 and was later made Director, retiring in 1950. He was an advocate of the "cure task" system, a graduated exercise program for patients as they began to improve.[32] He allowed recreational activities and trips off the hospital grounds. Not all physicians agreed with his system, but the *Journal of the Outdoor Life,* a periodical on tuberculosis founded by Dr. Lawrason Brown, published many articles on the rehabilitation going on at sanatoriums across the country.

Supposedly the patients at Ray Brook did not have advanced cases of tuberculosis (although there were some who did) which may explain the freedoms they enjoyed. Patients were also expected to do chores, especially being responsible for their own personal care and hygiene. Evelyn was expected to clean her own bed space. An inspector she jokingly calls *Johnnie Dust* would go around and check the rooms (February 16). At one point, when she was obviously slacking in her chores, Evelyn wrote that the nurse, Miss Martin, *raved at me! Good night! She scolded about everything under the sun, the floor most of all* (June 14). Public health experts reported that tuberculosis germs lurked in dust, so cleanliness was extremely important. Patients helped each other with chores. The nurse once asked another patient to make Evelyn's bed for her when she wasn't feeling well. The girls washed each other's hair, used the kitchen to make their own cocoa and snacks, and went to the laundry room to iron their own clothes.

There was an official "work list," which rotated periodically, of more general work at the sanatorium, such as food service chores and sorting the mail, to help defray the cost of their care. Patients apparently also received some pay for their work because Evelyn wrote: *I wish pay day would hurry up and come so I could get some stationery* (September 29). She mentioned several of her "jobs" at Ray Brook and liked some more than others. *I'm on mail again. Hooray!* (September 19). But she hated carrying milk. *Gee, I'm sick of carrying that big heavy can* (September 27). She did not have just one job at a time, either. At one point she was *on mail, cloakroom, and in bakery* (October 10). One of the girls did library work and Evelyn may have done that too, later on. Evelyn sometimes carried trays for bed patients. She wrote: *I have to take care of Mrs. Diamond this week* (July 13), and *Tillie's sick and Martin asked me to carry Mrs. Diamond's tray till she gets up* (October 25), and dispassionately, *I don't have to carry a tray anymore because Mrs. Senaday died* (January 9). Male patients had different jobs. Morris waited on tables in addition to leading religious services for the Jewish patients. Evelyn did learn some skills that she hoped would be useful after she recovered from tuberculosis. For instance, she noted in the diary that she *went to the office [to learn] to use the typewriter* (March 7).

A Losing Battle

Clearly, the hospital was concerned about too much activity causing a set-back in a patient's recovery because Evelyn did worry about getting into trouble for over-doing things. She once met Dr. Ryan (no relation to Helen Ryan) when she was out walking and she wrote: *I certainly did expect to be called over to the office and given a call down* and she was surprised when that did not happen (April 23). And she worried about her weight loss. Drinking a lot of milk between meals to gain weight was a standard part of the tuberculosis cure. The hospital got its milk from a nearby dairy farm in Ray Brook. Cows had to pass a tuberculin test because they could become infected and possibly pass on the disease to humans through milk. Evelyn wrote in the diary that she *started drinking milk again to see if I can't stop losing and gain some weight"* (April 5). Another April entry recorded her startling loss of 4 pounds.

From *Woodland Whispers* December, 1925

Evelyn moaned: *If they'd only give us some decent meals, maybe one could gain, but as it is—ugh* (April 18). Unfortunately, the war had caused food shortages and a need to conserve food at home in America. Meatless meals and food prepared with corn or oat flour instead of wheat were strongly encouraged. It surely would have been harder for tuberculosis patients to maintain their weight with the hospital affected by food shortages.

Evelyn continued to lose weight, an indication of her continuing illness. By May 23, her weight had dropped from 121½ to 115 pounds, then 114 pounds by mid-June. She reported having to take in the waist of her white flannel skirt by 2 inches. She wrote, with sarcasm: *Oh, I'm getting well so fast that my clothes are dropping off* (June 10). After her birthday in August, she gained 1½ pounds, and in October, weighed 116 pounds—better, but not yet normal for her. But a 2½ pound gain led her to write: *I'm getting so fat I don't know what to do* (November 14). At her last recording of her weight in the diary in November she weighed 121½ pounds and was beginning to think that was enough.

And she worried about fever. If Evelyn's temperature went up, she *cured like mad*, which helped: *Temp down* (September 7), and *Was in bed all day. My temp has gone down* (to 98 degrees from 100) (January 20-22). Staying in bed did seem to lower her temperature, but she dreaded taking it: *Didn't take it...because I don't want to know* (June 4). The consequence of fever would have been frustrating: more rest, less activity.

After suffering from a cold, Evelyn wrote that she was pretty mad because: *I got the lecture of my young life* from Morris who apparently scolded her for not resting. But she added: *I deserved it, but then we do not always like to hear the truth* (October 6). Evelyn actually suffered quite a lot during 1918. Any increased activity was likely to take a toll on her health, and she usually rested more when that happened. She said she *Ran every step of the way* to the railroad station to see three fellows off, then added: *I'm awfully sorry I did it now* (August 5). She recorded the really bad days: *Oh, Diary, I am one sick girl today* (June 2) and *Oh, Diary, I feel pretty punk tonight...I had chills and a headache. Just took a big dose of castor oil—ugh!* (July 30). Castor oil tasted horrible, but was another standard part of the tuberculosis treatment. Actually, many well people took castor oil as a health tonic. Later on at the hospital, it was mixed with tomato juice and was called a "Ray Brook Cocktail."

DIETARY

SUNDAY

Breakfast: Oranges, flaked wheat, boiled eggs, coffee cake, coffee, cocoa, milk.
Dinner: Tomato soup with rice, roast chicken with dressing, mashed potatoes, macaroni au gratin, celery, loganberry sherbet, vanilla layer cake, coffee, milk.
Supper: Sweet potatoes, rice with cream, pears, marble cake, tea, milk.
Lunches: Milk A. M. and P. M.

MONDAY

Breakfast: Grapes, yellow meal, boiled eggs, buttered toast, coffee, cocoa, milk.
Dinner: Chicken broth with rice, roast pork, mashed potatoes, apple sauce, corn, bread pudding, assorted nuts, tea, milk.
Supper: Broiled steak, baked potatoes, dill pickles, raised biscuit with maple syrup, tea, milk.
Lunches: Milk A. M. and P. M.

TUESDAY

Breakfast: Rolled oats, fried eggs, hot rolls, coffee, cocoa, milk.
Dinner: Tomato soup, roast lamb, boiled potatoes, creamed carrots, coldslaw, apple pie, tea, milk.
Supper: Frankfurters, potato salad, sugar cookies, grapes, tea, milk.
Lunches: Milk A. M. and P. M.

WEDNESDAY

Breakfast: Flaked wheat, fried bacon, buttered toast, orange marmalade, coffee, milk, cocoa.
Dinner: Bean soup, roast beef, mashed potatoes, sliced beets, creamed cauliflower, cream puffs, tea, milk.
Supper: Fried ham, mashed potatoes, sweet mixed pickles, canned plums, sponge cake, tea, milk.
Lunches: Milk A. M. and P. M.

THURSDAY

Breakfast: Apples, farina, boiled eggs, raised biscuit, coffee, cocoa, milk.
Dinner: Barley soup, beef loaf, boiled potatoes, mashed turnips, macaroni au gratin, cherry jello, tea, milk.
Supper: Fried lamb chops, baked potatoes, olives, French bread, grapes, tea, milk.
Lunches: Milk A. M. and P. M.

FRIDAY

Breakfast: Oranges, hominy, boiled eggs, corn cake, coffee, cocoa, milk.
Dinner: Clam chowder, boiled beef, canned salmon, boiled potatoes, lima beans, celery, lemon pie, tea, milk.
Supper: Baked mackerel, creamed potatoes, egg salad, pineapple, molasses cookies, tea, milk.
Lunches: Milk A. M. and P. M.

A later Ray Brook menu, when war shortages were over. From *Woodland Whispers* December, 1925

Evelyn had serious problems with her teeth, obvious from the start of the diary and throughout. Decayed teeth were a common problem in those days. Since we know now that eating sugar contributes to tooth decay, it is not hard to figure out why Evelyn had problems. It is obvious that she was eating a lot of candy, without realizing, perhaps, that the sugar was aggravating her tooth-aches. She said she had *punch and ice cream and stuff 'till I was sick* (May 15). Her suitors tied to win her heart with sweets. Charlie gave her a box of candy; Morris gave her Hershey bars and cake. On her birthday (August 20) she was given a cake and two boxes of candy. Morris even mailed her a cake when he was at home for a visit, then brought more candy to her when he returned! Evelyn loved her many treats. Toothpaste with fluoride didn't exist in those days and fluoride wasn't added to water until the 1940s, so it is no wonder there were so many bad teeth. And dental care was expensive.

By May, the pain in Evelyn's teeth became intolerable and she had to take a bus to see Dr. Oakey, a dentist in Saranac Lake. Her second appointment was extremely painful. There were no Novocain shots then. *Oh, but he hurt today! He tried to take the nerve out and it wasn't dead. Whew!* (June 6). Imagine a root canal today without Novocain! That wasn't the end of her ordeal, though. The dentist asked Dr. Bray, the superintendent at Ray Brook, to take an x-ray of her tooth so he could see the root. The sanatorium had x-ray technology before the dentist. Ray Brook got x-ray equipment in 1914. It was a valuable new diagnostic tool used to detect tuberculosis of the lungs. In August, Evelyn had two teeth pulled in Saranac Lake. This time, though, *He put cocaine[33] on so it didn't hurt much* (August 13). But the diary shows that she continued to have bad toothaches at least through September and must have run up a big dentist bill. She mentioned a figure of $25.00, a lot of money in 1918. Her teeth had to be treated because it was believed that severe dental problems caused fever and lowered resistance to tuberculosis. I wonder how the dentist pro-tected himself from contracting tuberculosis from patients. At one point, Eve-lyn's face became swollen and Dr. Ryan painted it (the skin) with iodine—a useless treatment but one that was tried with tuberculosis and other condi-tions at the time. The nurse sometimes put oil of cloves on her sore teeth to soothe the pain, which probably did help a bit.

Evelyn suffered from another medical complication during that year: a persis-tent sore throat. It is difficult to say whether this problem was related to her tuberculosis or not. In the spring, Dr. Bray had told her to whisper in order to rest her throat. The whisper order continued for weeks, and it was late June before Dr. Bray said she could use her voice a little. By the end of September, her throat hurt very badly again and she wrote: *My throat still has white spots on it* (October 2). I wonder if Evelyn may have had strep throat because a strep infection can cause white spots. Of course, there were no antibiotics then and strep infections sometimes progressed to rheumatic fever. It is also possible that she may have had tuberculosis of the throat. Parts of the body other than the lungs were sometimes affected by tuberculosis.

All the while, Evelyn continued with her work duties and took long walks out-doors, whispering instead of talking. When Dr. Bray told her again to *keep sort of quiet* Evelyn became impatient: *I can't be keeping quiet forever* (October 23). The most he could tell her was the throat irritation hadn't reached her vocal chords yet, and she was very unsettled: *It makes me nervous having a sore throat all the time* (November 6). During the celebration for the Armistice, her throat was just as sore as ever, and the diary ends without any resolution of that problem.

The Effect on Evelyn's Spirit

Evelyn certainly had fun, making friends and keeping busy while she was at Ray Brook, but her diary expresses a lot of anguish about having a very serious illness and being more or less confined to a hospital. She wrote, early in the diary: *I hate this place anyway* (January 20). And she was clearly discouraged: *I don't believe I'll ever get well* (January 31). By March, she was absolutely *sick and tired of this old place. Wish I could go home. If Dr. Bray*

Courtesy of Helen Ryan Garlock

doesn't hurry and give me my Special, I don't know what I'll do (March 11). Dr. Ryan examined her soon after and told her she was still "positive," not improving. When he told her it was uncertain whether she could go home in September, she became very, very homesick. Though she does not say so, she may have been hoping to return to school at the beginning of the next school year. Or maybe she had been told she would be sent away for a year to cure, and had that date in mind. I wonder if anyone ever had a talk with her about how long curing might realistically take. Her "Special" (physical examination) with Dr. Bray finally came on April 1, but that was when he told her to talk in a whisper. Dr. Bray spoke to her mother then, who told Evelyn what he had said. *He said I had an infiltration, whatever that might be* (April 2). Having an infiltration would seem to indicate that she had pneumonia. Even if she didn't understand it, Evelyn knew it wasn't a good sign. *The old TB seems to stick to me like a friend without any money* (April 10).

Evelyn did not mention the Trudeau Clinic of Doctors, pictured in Helen Ryan's photograph album. It seems to be a gathering of physicians and the word "Clinic" in Helen's handwriting implies that they may have come in from Trudeau Sanatorium to see patients at Ray Brook. The Clinic must have had some significance for Helen. It could have been comforting to have so much medical expertise on hand, but Evelyn was not comforted at all by her examinations by physicians.

Evelyn increased her time curing after the bad report in April, but remained cranky, sad and sick: *Cried a lot. Felt punk this afternoon, tried to cure in bed, but Miss Martin told me to go to Dr. Bray* (May 3). Willful once again, she didn't go. Instead, she wallowed in her sadness: *If only I could go home for a visit* (May 4). Pretty soon, a package came from home with all her old clothes in it, which only increased her homesickness and must have made her wonder where her "home" was. The clothes seemed like *old friends* and brought back memories. *I'd give the world if I were only well enough to go home*, she wrote (May 20). But Evelyn only got worse, and wrote that she had *terrible pleurisy. Miss Martin painted it with iodine* (on her chest) (June 5). Pleurisy caused coughing and pain around the lungs and could have been a side effect of pneumonia. Iodine would have done nothing to help.

Message No. 1

GOODCHEER

"be of good cheer"

The most cheerful optimist in my class at school was a boy with one leg. Nobody can be an optimist until he loses something worth while—*The Editor*

PUBLISHED BY
THE TROTTY VECK MESSENGERS
SARANAC LAKE, N.Y.

Evelyn was alarmed at her weight loss during this time, but tried to change her attitude: *Still, I'm not going to worry. That only makes things worse I guess. I'll get well if I stick at it long enough. If I do* (June 13). She underlined the last part twice, not quite resigned to do what it might take. Her feelings of sadness and frustration were understandable but keeping a positive attitude was considered critical in curing from tuberculosis. And she seemed to know this. She frequently added, after her complaints, *I should worry*, which I think is a Yiddish expression meaning "why should I worry?" or "what good does it do to worry?" Not long after Evelyn kept her diary, a patient curing in Saranac Lake named Beanie Barnet began

72

to publish a series of tiny pamphlets designed to cheer up people with dozens of meaningful quotations in each issue. They were called the *Trotty Veck Messages*. Dr. E.L. Trudeau had tried to teach his patients to accept their situation calmly so they could learn how to live with tuberculosis. After all, it was at best a chronic condition with no reliable cure at the time.

Perhaps Evelyn considered her sadness and frustration her *secrets*, best kept confined to her diary. She felt ashamed of her feelings. *Sat with Morris tonight, and I'm so ashamed of myself, Diary. I had the blues, or rather, I have the blues and I let it all out on him, but he's a peach. Was great to me.* (October 3). Some patients who had already passed their teenage years may have had an easier time dealing with the frustration and boredom of curing, some even welcoming the chance for peaceful reflection, but the problem was not uncommon. In the 1930s, a group of former patients formed the Saranac Lake Study and Craft Guild to try to address the problem of having too much time on one's hands leading to depression, by giving curing patients a sense of purpose through useful activity. The Guild tried to promote optimism in the face of illness: "The enforced leisure which is part of the long period of treatment...has proven to be a rich gift...to those who have never stopped to consider what they really wanted from life."[34] Many former patients have stayed on to live and work in Saranac Lake, believing that their lives had been changed for the better in this healing community.[35]

Evelyn, at sixteen, had not yet gained the degree of perspective that she may have achieved over time: *Oh, Diary, I want to go home so badly*, unable to conquer her homesickness. *I hope by September 1st I'll be able to go home. By the way things look now, I can't see as I'm one bit better than I was when I came. Still, I feel alright, so I'm thankful for that much* (July 1). So, she was able to think positively—a little. Of course, she knew that others were worse off that she was. And now it was summer, and she had met Morris. She had to whisper to him because of doctor's orders, but maybe that brought them closer together. Trying to be hopeful, she wrote: *There certainly is a small chance of me going home in September. Oh yes!* (July 28). Pretty soon, it was Evelyn's birthday and she had gained a little weight. She was a bit more cheerful, but still apprehensive about her next examination by the doctor: *I wonder if Dr. Bray is going to give me my Special. I'd like to know if I'm dead or alive or what* (August 22). Although there is no diary in which Helen Ryan expressed her emotions about having tuberculosis, her photograph album contains occasional clues. Her caption for the photograph below, "Dr. Bray gave them ninety

Dr. Bray gave them ninety days.

Courtesy of Helen Ryan Garlock

days," shows her ability to joke about the situation. It is a cute picture. Helen had a sense of humor, though I think this is a pretty dark example of humor, given the situation. The girls are politely smiling for Helen's camera, but they are not laughing with her. My sense of Helen, from her likenesses, is that she tried to stay cheerful and live her life to the fullest, but who knows. She may have had rough days, just as Evelyn did. And Helen had been at Ray Brook even longer than Evelyn.

Patients sometimes left the sanatorium when there was no longer any hope of a cure. It must have been awfully hard for Evelyn to say good-bye to her friend Tommy (a girl). *Poor kid. I hope she'll get along alright at home. It certainly is tough luck to get worse after coming here* (August 24). Probably Tommy went home to die, but Evelyn did not seem to want to believe it because home was a place where she longed to be well enough to go. When Morris made plans to go home for a holiday, she wrote: *I wish I had somewhere to go to* (August 25). *Oh, dear Diary, I'm just about sick and tired of the whole game. Just about disgusted as I can be. I don't believe I'll ever get one bit better than I am. I don't see the use of staying here* (August 26). Going home could mean you were better, or you were worse. Evelyn started to wonder if there was any point in staying if she wasn't getting well.

Evelyn's persistent fever was not a good sign. *Why, oh why doesn't it go down? Am I ever going to get well? I'm just about discouraged* (September 5). *Just cure and cure, all the time, except when at services* (September 6). She would miss her father's birthday in September—perhaps the main reason she wanted to be home by then. Her only face-to-face family contact was with her mother and she missed her father terribly. Fanny had written to Adolph, who was probably then at the Broome County sanatorium, asking him to get a *dress*

74

and slippers for Evelyn and he wrote back saying that he was not well enough to go to town. Evelyn said she didn't care, was just concerned for him (March 25). But happily, on March 29, the dress and shoes arrived in the mail. *I could just hug my Daddy for getting them* (March 29). He had managed somehow. When the spring violets bloomed, Evelyn picked a bunch and mailed them to her father. She knitted a sweater for him and mailed it for his birthday, which she missed.

Evelyn told her diary that she felt very ashamed for having *the blues.* Soon she had more reason to be hopeful about her health. *Had my Special today by Dr. Brown—my right lung is good and my left is improving. I don't feel as blue* (October 5). She had always been hanging her hopes on the "Special" examinations. But she saw no big reason to celebrate—she was still homesick. And the date (September) that she had anticipated going home had passed. *This darned old place gets on my nerves more and more & the people aren't near as decent as the bunch that was here last winter. But I'll stick it out anyway until Spring and then Ta Ta Ray Brook* (October 22). Evelyn had seen a lot of patients come and go in the year or so that she had been at the hospital. And still she waited.

The Diary Ends

Evelyn suddenly stopped writing in her diary after filling every single page daily from January 1 through November 18 of 1918. All of the remaining pages to the end of the year are blank. There is no way to know for sure why she stopped. She seemed to have been feeling better at that time but, of course, could have suffered a relapse. Curing from tuberculosis was not just a matter of steady improvement. There were bound to be ups and downs. Certainly, something serious prevented her from writing any more that year.

On the day after the parade celebrating the end of the war, Evelyn stated that they had started rehearsals for a "Thanksgiving stunt." She said it was going to be a school scene, entitled "School Days" and Evelyn would play the part of Mary Jane. On November 18, she took a walk with Helen and then went to rehearsal. At that point the diary ends. Was she too busy with the play to write? That seemed unlikely to me because she had never missed a day with her diary until then. And there are no photographs in Helen Ryan's album that are labeled "School Days." Both Helen and her sister Skip (Florence) were still at Ray Brook because they are mentioned in the diary just days before Evelyn stopped writing, so Helen would have had photographs of an event like that. Was it cancelled? I did a little more research in local records and newspapers on what I thought might be a clue to a possible cancellation of the play and the abrupt ending of the diary: the appearance of a new world epidemic, which was similar to the H1N1 epidemic in 2009, but different in that its effects were very deadly.

"Spanish Flu"

History Sidebar

The influenza virus of 1918, called "Spanish Flu," which was in the same category as the H1N1 virus, or "swine flu," spread so fast across the Unied States and affected so many people that it was the worst epidemic the country had ever seen. The effects are almost unimaginable. There was no vaccine. One fourth of the United States population died. Worldwide, the disease killed an estimated 50 million people, and probably more, about one fifth of the world's population. When the epidemic first hit the United States in the spring of 1918, it was a strain from which most people recovered, but the virus may have mutated in the fall when it became deadly. The lungs of some of the sufferers filled up with fluid, causing death within hours.

Tens of thousands of World War I servicemen died of influenza, and the movement of troops at war's end helped spread the disease. Researchers are still studying the epidemic today. There is a lack of good scientific data from the time and, during the war, some of the newspaper reporting was censored so that fighting troops did not appear vulnerable. Celebrations around the United States at war's end, like the one Evelyn attended, also spread the influenza virus through crowds that gathered. Soon public health officials limited gatherings and distributed masks they hoped would limit the spread of the disease. The Red Cross was already mobilized due to the war effort, but communities were overwhelmed by health care needs. Burials of the dead were held up because of large numbers of fatalities. The crisis in a given community lasted only a few weeks, however, and the *pandemic* (worldwide epidemic) began to slowly disappear from areas like New York State.[36]

What Research Revealed

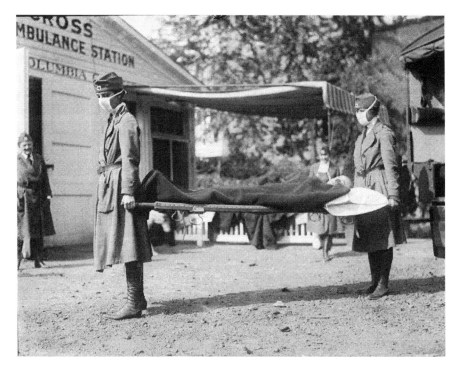

Demonstration at the Emergency Ambulance Station in Washington, D.C. during the Influenza pandemic of 1918. Courtesy of Library of Congress Digital Collection LC-DIG-npcc-18662

One Epidemic on Top of Another

The *Record Book of the Health Officer*, Dr. Charles C. Trembley of Saranac Lake, lists cases of influenza beginning in October of 1918. During that month, 419 cases were reported in the village. After a woman visiting her daughter in Saranac Lake died of influenza, nurses began a house-to-house survey supervised by the local Red Cross. A warning was issued by the New York State Commissioner of Health, Herman M. Biggs. The Commissioner listed typical symptoms along with warnings about contagion. "Like other infections of the respiratory tract influenza spreads from one individual to another by contact with the discharges from the nose and throat, scattered by coughing, sneezing, [etc]." Biggs stated that there was no known cure, just as there was no known cure for tuberculosis. He suggested resting in bed, and avoiding "badly aired" and crowded places. These precautions were very similar to those for tuberculosis. And, like tuberculosis, the disease was worse for young adults. Researchers now believe that the immune systems of the healthiest age groups over-reacted to the influenza virus, killing large numbers of victims whose lungs filled up with fluid (smothering them) as a result.

There was another, smaller wave of the epidemic in Saranac Lake in February of 1919, with 27 cases at Trudeau Sanatorium. The total number of cases in Saranac Lake over a 6 month period was 499, but only 3 deaths were recorded by the health officer, 2 of them visitors to the village, none at Trudeau.[37] It seems clear that Saranac Lake came through the ordeal pretty well. At the village of Lake Placid, just 10 miles away, it was a different story. The first report of influenza in the *Lake Placid News* occurred on September 27, 1918. The headline read: "Grippe Epidemic Is Nationwide." The October 11 issue reported that the board of health had closed schools, churches, the theater, and other place of public gatherings to stop the spread of the epidemic that had hit the village. One ominous headline read: "Several have succumbed." The outbreak had begun the previous week, and the *News* reported that "local physicians, nurses and pharmacies have since been working night and day to save patients." Up to that point, 10 obituaries had already been printed in the newspaper. By October 18, the situation had gotten out of control and an emergency hospital was set up in a hotel. A reporter noted, on October 18: "The death rate has exceeded anything in the history of the community." At least 32 people died in the small village of Lake Placid.

Likely, the situation in Saranac Lake was under better control because the Saranac Lake community was knowledgeable about contagious disease and its containment, having treated tubercular patients for years. Some people across the country in general, and in Lake Placid in particular, believed that tuberculosis patients had an inherited defect that made them more susceptible to the disease. The general public feared contagion and treated tuberculosis patients as outcasts. Signs such as "No Tuberculars Allowed" were posted in Lake Placid establishments. It has been said that drivers of cars passing through Saranac Lake held handkerchiefs over their faces to aviod breathing tuberculosis germs filling the ambient air, which we now know was ridiculous. But tuberculosis patients had been welcomed in Saranac Lake and that fact actually helped the village in terms of dealing with the influenza epidemic. The difference in the outcome of the epidemic makes this clear.

Saranac Lake was a community, not only of *tuberculars* (people suffering from tuberculosis), but of substantial numbers of care givers who knew how to deal with a communicable disease. Saranac Lake had a hospital, and a lot of physicians and nurses. Most importantly, Saranac Lake had been a pioneer in the field of public health. Village residents had been helping the sick for many years with very few of its care givers becoming ill.[38] After the Armistice, Saranac Lake was named a Home Sanatorium by the national Public Health Service, resulting in an influx of discharged servicemen and army nurses (250 by early 1920) infected with tuberculosis from all across the country.

Evelyn's diary does not tell us about Ray Brook's experience of the flu epidemic. She did mention once in her diary in September when Morris was sick in bed: *There's an epidemic going around* (September 21). It is possible that she may have heard something about the Spanish flu occurring somewhere, but she didn't name it. Her mother soon had an awful cold, then Evelyn. She wrote: *For a change, Diary, I've god ad orful gold id by ead. I can't talg straighd or adything* (October 5). She showed her sense of humor then, and soon recovered from her cold. Apparently, the others did as well. These dates coincide with the dates of the *Lake Placid News* stories about the flu epidemic, but the *epidemic* Evelyn mentioned might have been just a cold.

There may have been restrictions on large gatherings when the flu was at its peak locally. Ray Brook patients and personnel may even have been under quarantine, but Evelyn did not say so in the diary before its end. Ray Brook Hospital, like Trudeau Sanatorium, was pretty much a self-contained community which may have helped prevent the influenza virus from being brought in from outside. But it is hard to understand why patients were allowed out to participate in the armistice celebrations. Running off to the parades during a flu epidemic was extremely dangerous for people already suffering from lung disease. I had wondered if Evelyn had caught the flu and that is the reason the diary ended in November, but I found no evidence of it.

The only mention of influenza at the Ray Brook Hospital in the *Lake Placid News* occurred on January 13, 1919. The *News* reported that Ray Brook was under strict quarantine, with sixty cases of influenza at the hospital. This was a very serious situation. The *News* also reported three deaths at Ray Brook over the previous weekend, of patients age 33, 32, and 15 (Evelyn was then 17). This was just before a second wave of influenza hit Saranac Lake and Trudeau Sanatorium in February, but was not deadly there. It would have been very interesting to read a diary account of events at Ray Brook during the epidemic that hit there in January.

After the Diary's End

If Evelyn had influenza while at Ray Brook, she did not die from it. No existing records tell whether she had the flu or how long she was a patient at Ray Brook Hospital, but she definitely did not say *Ta ta Ray Brook* in the spring. The U. S. Census shows that she was still a patient at Ray Brook in January of 1920, and Fanny was still employed there as a waitress. At that point, they had been at Ray Brook for over two years. Only a very small percentage of patients stayed that long (see chart from *Woodland Whispers*, December 1925, when length of stay may have been even shorter). There is a possibility, of course, that Evelyn did go home for a time. She could even have been called home in November of 1918 when she stopped writing in her diary, but came back. I hope that she was able to see her dad sometime.

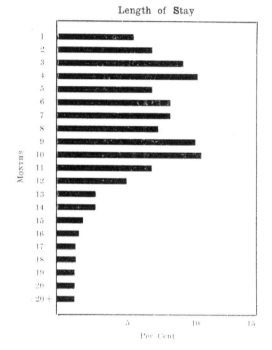

Life at Ray Brook stayed pretty much the same in the 1920s. The pamphlet called *Woodland Whispers*, published periodically by patients, indicates that Minstrel Shows, Halloween parties, ball games, etc. continued. This periodical also carried news from former patients and mentioned a planned reunion, which is evidence of the lasting friendships patients formed.

Helen Ryan was not among the patients listed at Ray Brook in the 1920 Census. She appears to have been there in 1919, because of dates on some of the photographed events in her album. One photo lists names and death dates of friends in the photo, written in her white ink. It must have been a struggle to remain hopeful of a cure while other young people were dying around them. Evelyn rarely mentioned death in her diary, but it must have lurked in her mind.

Courtesy of Helen Ryan Garlock

I believe Helen stayed at least through October of 1919 because there is a photograph in her album which she labels a Halloween event. People are in costume, but not the gingham aprons Evelyn said they wore for Halloween in 1918. In the photograph, a sign reads: "A Teacher's Dream at Ray Brook" and there in the group is Evelyn wearing a little girl dress and a large bow in her hair, right next to Helen. The caption in Helen's handwriting under the photograph states that Helen played Buster Brown. With a little research I found out that Buster Brown was a character in a popular comic strip originating in 1902 and that Buster Brown had a sister named Mary Jane. Evelyn wrote in the diary that she would play Mary Jane in the "School Days" Thanksgiving skit planned for 1918, so this could be that skit, postponed and renamed "A Teacher's Dream." Helen was supposed to play Buster Brown's dog, Tige in "School Days." Or they could have recycled costumes from last Thanksgiving for "A Teacher's Dream," or Helen could even have possibly mislabeled the photograph as a "Halloween Festival."

Halloween Festival

A TEACHER'S DREAM AT RAYBROOK

A Regular Night Mare play given by girls of East Wing — Florence Guthrie Irwin — Helen and Buster Brown

Buster Brown (Helen) and Mary Jane (Evelyn) are arm in arm on the left side of the photograph above. The girls had been friends for a long time at Ray Brook. Sadly, like Evelyn's friend Tommy, Helen did not get better at Ray Brook and returned to her home to spend her last days with her widowed father who had left the farm and

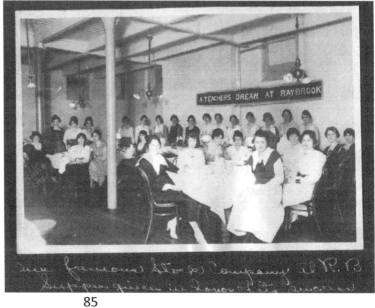

Helen & her dad. Courtesy of Helen Ryan Garlock

moved to the village of Newport, New York. Helen slowly wasted away and died there in 1921. This wasting away is why, as noted, tuberculosis was often called "consumption." The family plot at the cemetery where Helen was buried is marked by a classic statue of a lovely young woman, a fitting tribute to the beloved youngest daughter who never recovered from tuberculosis. Perhaps Evelyn received news of Helen's death in a letter. Helen's sister Skip (Florence) recovered and became a working woman. Mrs. Helen Garlock, the daughter of one of Helen Ryan's brothers, named for her aunt, told me that Florence died in 1968 of an apparent relapse of tuberculosis. It was not unheard of to have a relapse after such a long span of relatively good health. Another Ryan sibling, Henry, had died of pneumonia in 1919.

Author photographs.

86

Still another brother, William J. Ryan, was inspired to pursue medicine, worked in pulmonary research, and joined the anti-tuberculosis crusade. William Ryan graduated from Albany Medical College in 1915 (incidentally, the year that the famous Dr. E.L. Trudeau died at Saranac Lake). Dr. Ryan served as an intern and resident physician, and then entered the U.S. Army Medical Corps during World War I. After he returned from the war, he began to specialize in pulmonary diseases during a residency at the New York City municipal sanatorium at Otisville, New York. Mrs. Garlock believes that her uncle abandoned his plan to become a general surgeon after his sisters became ill and, instead, chose to undertake a long career of combatting tuberculosis.

By 1920, Dr. Ryan had become Director of the TB Division of the U.S. Veteran's Bureau in New York City. On November 1, 1921, soon after his sister Helen's death, Dr. Ryan was named Director of the Rockland County Sanatorium at Summit Park, New York. He also served terms as president of the Sanatorium Superintendent's Association East, and as president of the American Trudeau Society.[39] Although it was not possible for him to have saved his sister Helen, he helped countless other tuberculosis patients and worked to eradicate the disease.

Dr. William Ryan & family. Courtesy of Helen Ryan Garlock

The sanatorium at Summit Park had been built in 1919, and Dr. Ryan oversaw the addition of a new facility in 1936, with the aid of the Works Progress Administration. He performed an operation there called artificial *pneumothorax* (collapsed lung) on some of his patients, as did some other surgeons treating tuberculosis in Saranac Lake and across the country. At the time, it was believed that collapsing a lung surgically would allow it to rest and therefore heal. Pneumothorax was considered the first useful treatment that went beyond the simple rest

INFECTION BY INHALATION—Krause
FREE TUBERCULOSIS DISPENSARIES—Pritchard
OPEN-AIR SCHOOL—Jackson
TEN PREACHMENTS ON WORRY—Cuebas

PUBLISHED MONTHLY IN THE INTEREST OF THE
ANTI-TUBERCULOSIS CAMPAIGN
381 FOURTH AVE., NEW YORK CITY
15 CENTS A COPY $1.50 A YEAR

Helen Ryan Courtesy of Helen Ryan Garlock

cure. Dr. Ryan remained as Superintendent at Summit Park until his sudden death of a heart attack in 1942.

Dr. Ryan saw promise in the idea of early diagnosis of tuberculosis and advocated particularly for examination of school children. He undoubtedly wished that his own sisters had had earlier care. There was research that showed that children in a family where tuberculosis was present were twenty times more likely to get sick. Some children were separated from a parent with tuberculosis, unlike Evelyn, apparently. A 1907 article in the *Journal of the Outdoor Life* had recommended that "The healthy children of tuberculous parents should be entirely removed (when possible) from the tuberculous environment, sent to boarding school during the winter months and a long vacation away from the family in the summer." Probably very few families could afford to follow this advice, or wished to be separated from their children.

Fresh Air Schools were set up in a few locations, where children were placed in an outdoor environment during school hours (see sidebar following). Dr. Ryan and some other physicians believed that very young children had some natural resistance to tuberculosis germs. "Although we find evidences of infection, younger children do not break down. But from adolescence on, particularly in girls, resistance is weakened," he said.[40] If only Helen had been examined and diagnosed earlier...but he seemed to think girls were more susceptible.

Fresh Air Schools

History Sidebar

Fresh Air Schools" started popping up across the country as part of the anti-tuberculosis crusade. Sometimes called "Open Air Schools," and started in Europe, they were designed to promote children's health. Obviously, the focus was on exposing pupils to as much fresh air as possible, either with classes being held outdoors, or in rooms with wide open windows. The children had to bundle up to keep warm in winter. The first fresh air school in the United States opened in Providence, Rhode Island, at about 1907 or 1908, and another opened in New York City very soon after. Some of these schools were for children already sick with tuberculosis, and others were primarily aimed at prevention.

A 1916 tuberculosis directory indicated that, by that time, there were at least one thousand fresh air schools, fresh air classes and fresh air rooms in schools for children suffering from tuberculosis, and hundreds more for healthy children. Under medical supervision at the fresh air schools, children were watched for any signs of ill health and were carefully supervised in maintaining "perfect hygiene, good food, rest, play, study and exercise" in as "homelike" a setting as possible.

In 1916, most of the fresh air schools in New York State were located in larger cities, but Saranac Lake had one. The tuberculosis directory listed: "Fresh Air Room, Main Street School (September 3, 1912), Capacity: 15; Medical Director: Dr. S.W. Outwater; Supported by public tax." The date 1912 was probably the date the room first opened up. This special room was publically supported and most likely would have been used by the children of tuberculosis patients coming to Saranac Lake to cure. Another open air school was located at Stony Wold Sanatorium at nearby Lake Kusuaqua.[41]

Open Air Class on Day Camp Rutherford (ferry boat); Manhattan across the river. Courtesy of Library of Congress Digital Collection LC-USZ62-120423

Saranac Lake physicians had been advocates for child health measures and began a course of lectures in 1908 for school children from sixth grade through high school, arranged through the Saranac Lake Society for the Control of Tuberculosis. Cleanliness and fresh air were emphasized in lessons for school children. An exhibit with doll house size sleeping rooms was set up to teach them the difference between a healthy and an unhealthy bedroom.[42]

Snack time at Saranac Lake's Fresh Air Room. Courtesy of the Adirondack Collection, Saranac Lake Free Library 99.152K

A Family of Two

Evelyn undoubtedly lost many friends to tuberculosis, but the loss of her father must have been the hardest to bear. We can only hope that Evelyn was able to visit her father before he died at the Broome County Tuberculosis Hospital at Chenango, on February 14, 1924.[43] Of course, she must have been heart-broken at the news of his death and would be reminded every Valentine's Day. Evelyn and Fanny stayed on at Ray Brook after that. According to the New York State Census of 1925, Fanny was still working there as a laundress, a typically exhausting and low-paying job. At that time, married women had not generally worked outside the home, but a widow or a woman whose husband was incapacitated, and also many women of the working class simply had to work. Fanny had been in that category for years.

Unidentified laundry workers at Ray Brook Courtesy of the Adirondack Collection, Saranac Lake Free Library 86.596K

Evelyn was no longer listed as a patient on the 1925 New York State Census. She must have regained her health somewhat because she was employed at Ray Brook as a *stenographer* (a person who took dictation in shorthand), another typically low-paying job. Office work that previously had been men's work was opening up for women but at lower wages. Women's wages were low, no matter what the job, but Evelyn and Fanny must have been grateful for whatever work they could find. At least they were both earning a little money at the place that had now become their home without Adolph.

More women than ever before entered the work force during and after World War I because of a boom in the economy, with women earning less than men for the same job. Women did mostly office work, unskilled factory work, service jobs, teaching and nursing. After the war, working women began returning to the home. Homemaking was once again considered the most suitable occupation for a married woman. Women were still struggling for rights, and were not allowed to vote in national elections until the Nineteenth Amendment was passed in 1920. By 1925, women had gained some rights, but a family without a male provider suffered economically. With stenographer and laundress among the lowest paying jobs, Evelyn and Fanny could not have been well off financially.

The Ray Brook Hospital had housing for its employees. Former patients were often hired at sanatoriums. One reason was that the general public was afraid of contagion. One of Evelyn's fellow patients, a friend mentioned in the diary, Anna Sanlow, was hired by Dr. Bray as his x-ray technician, a job she held for many years. He said he was impressed with the fine quality of her craft work, her knitting, for example, and thought she would be a good worker.[44]

Evelyn must have "broken down" again with tuberculosis and wound up as a patient in a cure cottage in Saranac Lake. The name Bellak appears in a record that was kept of the disinfection procedures that took place every time a patient vacated a room or died at a cure cottage. I have read that carbolic acid or formaldehyde and lime were used for this purpose. Evelyn would have had to pay for her care at a cure cottage, and may have no longer qualified for state care. But based on her experience working at Ray Brook, Fanny Bellak took advantage of an opportunity to run a cure cottage in Saranac Lake herself, with Evelyn curing in it. This would have been a good way to provide for Evelyn's care and to earn extra money by caring for other patients. Running cure cottages was a thriving business in Saranac Lake and Fanny would have been very familiar with the process of curing.

Anna Sanlow at an x-ray machine. Courtesy of the Adirondack Collection, Saranac Lake Free Library. Ray Brook Album

Fanny started at a cottage located at 13 Riverside Drive (now 32 Kiwassa Road), at least as early as July, 1926. She wisely lowered the room rent on the recommendation of the Saranac Lake Society for the Control of Tuberculosis, though the TB Society thought the prices were still too high in 1926, because the three rooms were so small. As of May 1, 1928, the records show a move of the Bellak Cottage to a building at 3 Kiwassa Road (now 164 Kiwassa Road). Occasionally, cottage names changed as the proprietors moved. Miss Mary C. Mullin, R.N., social worker for the TB Society, visited on May 7 and reported: "House a little crowded, 2 beds in some rooms that are not large enough. Mrs. Bellak will change this; she has been in business before, having had a house at 13 Riverside Drive." Private sanatoriums (cure cottages) were licensed by the Board of Health. In March of 1929, the Bellak Cottage moved again across town to 4 Park Place. The Bellak Cottage on Park Place remained in her charge until October, 1931.[45] (Park Place is now named Prescott Place, but the building is gone.)

It is possible that Evelyn helped Fanny with the cure cottage operation, if she was well enough. Clearly, her health eventually improved enough that she was able to head downtown to find a job. The 1930 U.S. Census shows that Evelyn was the assistant librarian at the Saranac Lake Free Library. She would have had only a short walk to work from Park Place, but a steep climb going back home, unless she was able to afford a taxi. Stella C. Norton, the librarian, included this sentence in her end of the year report for 1929. "Much of the success of the year's work is due to our helpful and efficient assistant, Miss Evelyn Bellak, whose good work we appreciated highly." Wow, having a nice job, even part time, in the real world outside the sanatorium must have felt great!

The library was linked to the tuberculosis industry in Saranac Lake, taking orders from patients by phone for books. Someone (Evelyn?) took the time and gave some thought to picking out appropriate books for each patient. It was easier, the report said, now that they also had someone with an automobile to deliver books to bed patients. There was a small fee which had to be increased a bit to pay for wear and tear on the automobile. During the year 1929, 1356 deliveries were made to patients.

Evelyn had had some previous library experience as a volunteer story hour reader for young children at the Endicott Library in 1916, in the afternoons after school. She must have loved the library then and may have also worked at the library at Ray Brook while she was a patient. In Saranac Lake, Evelyn paid $1.00 out of her salary for a membership in the library and I'll bet she loved working there. But disappointment reared its ugly head again when Evelyn's illness returned. The librarian's report for 1930 reads: "We were very sorry to lose Miss Bellak from the library on account of ill health. She had given excellent service.[46] The last mention of the Bellak Cottage in the disinfection records was dated 1931, and the cottage at 4 Park Place was renamed the Morrison Cottage in 1932. I wondered what had happened to the Bellaks. There were no more New York State censuses taken after 1925 and, at the time of my research, the 1940 U.S. Census had not yet been released to the public. Evelyn's story stopped suddenly again, begging the question once more: did she die after her health broke down again?

Saranac Lake Free Library, before the addition. Courtesy of the Adirondack Collection, Saranac Lake Free Library 83.547

Saranac Lake Cure Cottages

History Sidebar

The village of Saranac Lake today is packed with closely spaced homes that once housed tuberculosis patients. Porches sprout in all directions on former cure cottages where patients once rested and slept in fresh outdoor air while reclining in bed or on a cure chair. Nearly 200 structures in Saranac Lake are now listed on the National Register of Historic Places and more are eligible. The cottages are a reminder of Saranac Lake's most important industry, now shut down.

Most of the cure cottages were run by women, often wives of patients or mothers, such as Fanny Bellak, of children with tuberculosis. There was so much demand for boarding the sick people who arrived on train after train to Saranac Lake that many families took a patient or two into their own homes, and added on cure porches. Dr.

Lawrason Brown had rules and guidelines for setting up an appropriate cure porch. Wealthier patients built fine homes for themselves and their families.

The Saranac Lake Society for the Control of Tuberculosis kept a registry and did inspections of cure cottages that rented out rooms to patients. After a private sanatorium was inspected and approved by the Society, it was licensed by the Board of Health. The TB Society was founded in 1907 as a "welfare organization" and "to safeguard and benefit the community of Saranac Lake." Miss Mullin reported, in 1930, that patients' insisting on staying in Saranac Lake even though they had no money to pay for their treatment, was becoming an increasing problem. They refused to go home because they did not want to return to unhealthy living conditions. The TB Society had an emergency fund and nurses who worked for lower than usual pay. They also provided "entertainment for patients such as motoring, boating, dinners, Rotary play, vaudeville show, and movies," and holiday activities, such as a Christmas party for the Fresh Air School.[47]

A cure cottage or a commercial private sanatorium operated as a business and proprietors frequently rented buildings, rather than owning. Some were run as "nursing cottages" in which patients were "on trays," meaning that their meals were brought to them in bed. Others were "ambulatory cottages" at which patients were well enough to walk to meals in a dining room downstairs or sometimes in an adjacent building.

There were cottages that catered to specific ethnic groups such as Greeks, Cubans, Blacks and Jewish people, and to specific industrial workers such as telephone workers, and shoe factory workers, specifically Endicott Johnson employees, who occupied two different cottages in Saranac Lake.[48] So there were many others from Evelyn's home town who came later to cure. Having something in common helped patients to adjust to being away from home, and cure porches were a place to socialize and watch the goings-on in the neighborhood.

A New Chapter

In trying to answer the question of whether Evelyn died in 1930, I did not find a death record for either Evelyn or Fanny in the Index of New York State Vital Records. These records had been released to the public only up to the 1950s. But I did discover that Evelyn's life story had an interesting new chapter when I found something else in the Index of Vital Records: a marriage record.

Not surprisingly, the new chapter in Evelyn's life involved a new boyfriend. Back on July 27, 1926, a fellow named Michael Hayes, age 29, had arrived at Saranac Lake with *incipient* (beginning) tuberculosis. He was examined on that date by Dr. Lawrason Brown and sent to 13 Riverside Drive, the Bellak Cottage.[49] He met Evelyn; they fell in love, and were later married on July 6, 1931 at the North Elba Town Hall in Lake Placid.

Finding the marriage record for Evelyn in the Index of Vital Records was a major discovery and I was happy to learn that Evelyn had finally found the right man, but I was confused about the details of the marriage. It seemed like a "quick" marriage ceremony held on a Monday after the Fourth of July holiday, at the Town Hall in Lake Placid, not Saranac Lake, where Evelyn was living. Perhaps they did not want to have the stigma of Saranac Lake's association with tuberculosis written on their marriage license. Being known to have tuberculosis did have consequences for individuals returning home and seeking jobs. Two clerks who worked at the Town Hall were listed as witnesses, not Fanny. I wondered: did they get married without telling Fanny? At the time of their marriage, Evelyn was nearly thirty years old and Michael was thirty-four. If Fanny had disapproved, it surely would have been because of Evelyn's fragile health, not her age. And a bigger question was: where did they go then? I was already pretty sure none of them stayed in Saranac Lake, but at the time of my research, it would be a few years before the next census, the 1940, would be released.

According to the marriage records, when Michael returned to Saranac Lake for Evelyn and married her in Lake Placid, he was a resident of Staten Island and

13 Riverisde Drive, today. Author photograph

worked at a printing press in Brooklyn. He had been cured and gone back to work. I decided to do a little research on Michael since I had his date of birth and I got lucky, quickly finding him in the 1930 U.S. Census living on Staten Island with his parents. I also found out from the Social Security Death Index that he had died in 1976 at the age of seventy-nine. Tuberculosis had not cut his life short, but what about Evelyn who was then Evelyn Hayes? She had outlived her friend Helen by over ten years, but her health had been failing when she left her job at the library in 1930. No more information about Evelyn turned up quickly like it had for Michael. Married women are harder to research in general, and Evelyn no longer had an unusual name like Bellak.

I was able to find a little more information on Michael. Michael was born in Brooklyn and grew up there. He was a second generation Irish American; all of his grandparents were born in Ireland. And all of the men in the family, including Michael, worked as *pressmen* (operators of a printing press) for New York City newspapers. Irish...a mixed marriage...Evelyn was Jewish and Michael was an Irish Catholic. Perhaps Fanny had disapproved. Was that why she had not been a witness at the marriage? There was no way I could answer that question, and maybe I was just being suspicious. Maybe she just couldn't get away from her cure cottage responsibilities.

"Guardian Angel"

My research floundered for a while, until I was able to travel to the area near Binghamton, New York where Evelyn had lived. I located the cemetery where her father Adolph was buried. I thought perhaps there would be some clues on his gravestone. And the Broome County Library was in Binghamton. There would be records to search there.

At the Jewish cemetery in Johnson City, near Endicott, I learned the final chapter of Evelyn's story. To the right of a large decorated stone monument that read "Adolph Bellak, beloved husband of Fanny Bellak," was a small, very plain stone marker. Although it had seemed like a long shot that Evelyn might be buried in Johnson City, I found her there. Carved on the small stone were the words: "DAUGHTER EVELYN AUG 20, 1901. MCH 12, 1932." I was disappointed to learn that Evelyn had not had a long and happy life with Michael, but not really surprised. She had left her work at the library in Saranac Lake because of "ill health," after all. At the time of her death at the age of 31, she had spent half of her life battling tuberculosis, ultimately a losing battle.

Author photograph

The discovery of Evelyn's grave, like so many other bits of information I had gleaned through my research, led to more questions. Was Evelyn's disease so bad that she learned she would not have long to live, and is that why Michael came for her, so they could spend her last days together? And what happened to Fanny? I wondered was she buried with her family, but no one was left to pay for a gravestone? I was able to find a partial answer to the last question at a monument store across from the cemetery, where there was a map. There were four graves under Bellak ownership in the cemetery plot, but only two were occupied. That left open the question of what happened to Fanny. I thought she was Jewish. If she hadn't been, would she not have been allowed to be buried there? Of course, she could have remarried after 1930, but she would have been about sixty years old by then.

Author photo

Courtesy of Don Morgan

At this point, standing there in the cemetery, I felt as though I had just found Evelyn. She was physically there, or her remains were, and yet, of course, she was gone. And I thought about the long battle for her life that she had fought and lost. I had heard of a Jewish custom of leaving a small stone on a gravestone as a sign that someone had come to visit. As I placed my stone, I wondered how many years it had been since Evelyn and Adolph had had any visitors. And I also thought about how much she loved her Daddy.

Since I now knew Evelyn's date of death, I was able to find her obituary in *The Binghamton Press*, dated March 14, 1932, on microfilm at the Broome County Library:

MRS. EVELYN BELLAK HAYES

Mrs. Evelyn S. Bellak Hayes, daughter of Mrs. Fannie Bellak, formerly of Saranac Lake, and now of South Orange, N.J., died Saturday night at 10:30 o'clock at South Orange. The body will arrive at 8:05 o'clock tonight on the Lackawanna and will be taken to the Roberts & DeMunn funeral home.

"...now of South Orange, N.J...."? Why was there no mention of Michael in this obituary? The Lackawanna was the railroad that went to Binghamton. Evelyn's burial and funeral were delayed because of the transportation, not in accordance with Jewish custom of burial before sundown.

I later found another obituary in the *New York Times* with the same date, but with slightly different details.

Hayes—At her home, 204 Fairview Ave., South Orange, N.J. on Saturday, March 12, 1932. Evelyn Bellak, beloved wife of Michael H. Hayes and daughter of the late Adolph and Mrs. Fannie Rothstein Bellak, in her thirty-second year.

Michael may have written this version, and perhaps Fanny wrote the other. But I wondered why they were living in South Orange, New Jersey at the time of Evelyn's death. This story was not yet complete by any means. Of course, I knew I could never make it really complete, but maybe I could eventually find out a little more.

Michael left no descendants, only a second wife, now deceased, so the trail had gone cold. I tried for a very long time to find a descendant of Michael's siblings. All of my letters were returned unopened by the post office. I was about to give up when I found an obituary of a niece who had been mentioned in Michael's obituary. Margaret Neumann was the daughter of Michael's brother Patrick Hayes. Her obituary listed a daughter, Patricia Powers, living in Saratoga County, New York. I sent off one more letter explaining my project and very quickly received a phone call from Patricia. During our conversation, she told me that Michael "loved Evelyn deeply and kept her close in his heart 'till the day he died," even though his second wife was also very special to him. Patricia remembers asking, as a young child, her Aunt Tess (Michael's second wife Theresa) why Uncle Mike said prayers every night for someone named Evelyn.

105

Evelyn. Courtesy of Patricia Powers

"Who was Evelyn?" she asked. Aunt Tess replied that Evelyn was his "guardian angel." Aunt Tess loved him enough to understand about Evelyn and informed Patricia that Evelyn "watches over him." The photograph is the only one found by Patricia that was identified as Evelyn. She is shown with an unknown male and she looks older and very thin so it may have been taken towards the end of her life. Her cause of death was "pulmonary tuberculosis and asphicsia" (lack of oxygen).[50]

Michael's obituary had mentioned that he was a World War I veteran and Patricia told me that he was in the Navy. I learned from the New York State Archives that Michael Hayes enlisted in the Navy in New York City on April 20, 1917 just two weeks after the United States entered the war. He was 20 years of age at the time. In August of 1917, he was assigned to Armed Draft Detail, which entailed stopping men on the street of New York City and de-manding to see their draft card. Since the war effort would require many more armed forces, the Selective Service Act of May 18, 1917 required that all men between the ages of 21 and 30 (later changed to between 18 and 45) register for the draft. Service men, such as Michael, were assigned to find slackers who were trying to avoid the draft. Then in October, having been promoted to Seaman's rank, he boarded the *SS Henry R. Mallory*, and served out the rest of the war transporting Army troops to fight in Europe, and then bringing them back when the war was over.

Navy Transport Ships in World War I

History Sidebar

The *SS Henry R. Mallory*, like many other merchant ships, was refitted for the Navy to carry large numbers of fighting troops across the Atlantic. Sleeping berths for soldiers and guns to fight off attacks by German U-boats were installed at the Brooklyn Navy Yard. U-boats had been sinking merchant ships at that time. The *Mallory's* first voyage began on June 14, 1917, heading for Brest, France. Michael Hayes was not on that first voyage. His tour of duty began in August, 1917. The *Mallory*, within the New York Division of Transport Force, made six trips to Europe before the Armistice was signed on November 11, 1918, carrying a total of 9756 passengers. The ships were always in

SS Mallory. Courtesy of Patricia Powers

danger of torpedo attacks and sailed in a convoy which included destroyers. The deck was manned at all times by numerous sailors assigned to watch with binoculars for submarine periscopes. Daily "abandon ship" drills were held. The ships steered a course of constant zigzagging to avoid attack. These maneuvers had to be coordinated by the clock to avoid a collision with another convoy ship, since radio communication would have been detected. Fortunately, ships travelled at a faster speed than subs. Camouflage painted on the ships made it harder for the enemy to calculate speed and course. The

Mallory got through the war unscathed, though a report from the ship came in on April 4, 1918 at 11:45 AM: "Attack defeated by gun fire and maneuver." At the end of the war, troops had to be transported back home, and the *Mallory* made seven more trips carrying 12,143 passengers, 2371 of whom were sick or wounded. Its total war time passenger count was over 21,000 and the last arrival date back in New York City was August 29, 1919.[51]

So this is what Michael was doing during the same time that Evelyn was curing at Ray Brook and helping to support the war effort. The Spanish flu epidemic also impacted the transport ships, which turned into floating hospitals as a result. Sick soldiers were refused transport before they boarded, but within a couple of days at sea, many more became sick and the crowded conditions increased contagion. Reminiscent of the TB cure, in a situation where over 500 men became ill aboard ship, "the soldiers were kept in the open air as much as possible, while boxing bouts, band concerts and other amusements on deck were conducted to keep up morale."[52] The shipboard epidemic played itself out, but many deaths occurred. Burial at sea was carried out as a solemn and dignified ritual.

Michael Hayes, aboard ship. Courtesy of Patricia Powers

Michael Hayes was discharged from the Navy on February 14, 1919. Patricia Powers told me that his black hair had turned white during the war. I learned that after Evelyn's death, because of his enduring affection for Evelyn, Michael also had a bond with her mother, who outlived Evelyn into the 1950s. Pat remembers that Uncle Mike sent money every month for years to Fanny Bellak, possibly for the rest of her life. That was heart-warming to hear. Fanny would have been his caretaker at his cure cottage at 13 Riverside Drive in Saranac Lake, and he was undoubtedly grateful for her role in his recovery. After searching records for some time, I learned that Fanny died at a home for the aged located at 121 West 105th

Street in New York City on January 2, 1957, at 89 years of age. She was buried at the Mount Richmond Cemetery on Staten Island, among the graves of large numbers of New York's immigrant populace. I wondered: did no one know there was room for her in the family plot with her husband and daughter? Michael Hayes remarried, had no children and died of a stroke in 1976 at the age of 79.[53]

And that is the end of the story at this point. I recognize that though my work has come to an end in writing this book, the story is necessarily incomplete. I believe there could be other family members who might be able supply details. Evelyn mentioned in her diary an "Uncle Wald" and an "Aunt Cella" whom I was unable to trace. Fanny Bellak's burial record lists a Mrs. Helen Hogan of New York City as a cousin. Is this the Helen who sewed clothes for Evelyn and mailed them to Ray Brook? Other questions also remain unanswered. Even though I have not quite figured it all out, it has been a joy for me to research Evelyn's story, getting to know her and also Helen Ryan through her photographs. In the process of my research, Evelyn, in particular, became quite like a friend I truly cared about. And I have enjoyed acting as a detective, finding traces of her life and attempting to put them all together like a jigsaw puzzle. Pat Powers told me that I had solved a mystery for her: why there had been resentment toward Uncle Mike by some family members. She believes it was because he married outside of the Catholic Church, a fact she hadn't known before.

I am grateful that Evelyn, or someone who cared about her, left behind, at the library, her little diary which she titled: "FOND MEMORIES OF RAY BROOK." And I am grateful that many people, like Helen Ryan's family, see the value in preserving these sorts of artifacts. The Adirondack Research Room at the Saranac Lake Free Library is a treasure trove of donations like these. And I believe that we are all helped in understanding history through the personal experiences, both ordinary and extraordinary, of these two young women and others who impacted their lives.

Epilogue

Unfortunately, Evelyn did not live long enough to try the drug therapies that were developed in the following decades. Was Evelyn helped by the rest cure? Probably--because she lived for about sixteen years with the disease. Could she have helped herself if she had rested more? Maybe—but Evelyn did not have a personality that would allow her to give up on living life to the fullest extent possible. The drug streptomycin came along in the 1940s and helped patients, but did not eradicate the disease because it allowed drug-resistant strains of the tuberculosis bacteria to develop. Other drugs were tried, but the most effective one was isoniazid, developed in the early 1950s. Few patients were left in Saranac Lake after that and Trudeau Sanatorium closed in 1954. The Sanatorium's endowment was used to establish a biomedical research facility, The Trudeau Institute, which continues its ground breaking work today. There has been a resurgence of tuberculosis in recent decades in cities in the United States (about 25,000 new cases per year) and even more in developing countries. New cases number about 8 million per year worldwide. An aggressive highly drug-resistant case was diagnosed in a patient in the United States in 2009, with no cure for this strain.[54] The Trudeau Institute is actively working to develop both a better influenza vaccine that will protect against multiple strains and a vaccine against drug resistant strains of tuberculosis.[55]

The Ray Brook State Hospital, the last of the local sanatoriums to close, reduced its bed capacity in the 1960s but continued in operation until 1971, when it was turned into a drug rehabilitation center for women. That facility closed in the winter of 1975-76 and since then the property has housed a New York State correctional facility. Saranac Lake's economy suffered greatly after the closing of Trudeau Sanatorium and it took a long while to recover. The TB Society still exists as The Saranac Lake Voluntary Health Association, offering medical equipment on loan, a visiting nurse service and a dental hygiene program, without charge. The grounds of the Sanatorium were taken over by the American Management Association. A bronze statue of Edward Livingston Trudeau and the tiny cure cottage "Little Red" were moved to the grounds of the Trudeau Institute. Dr. Trudeau's Saranac Laboratory was recently renovated by Historic Saranac Lake. Along with the office of Historic Saranac

Lake, a variety of exhibits commemorating the history of Saranac Lake's involvement in curing tuberculosis and in World War I, etc. have been open to the public. Historic Saranac Lake has a website with a great deal of historical information. Just around the corner from the Laboratory is the Saranac Lake Free Library which houses the Adirondack Research Room with an extensive collection of historical records on tuberculosis and Adirondack history. Their web site lists the tuberculosis materials they hold.[56] The Village of Saranac Lake is still packed with preserved former cure cottages and large segments of its population are descended from former patients and care givers who chose to remain in this healing community.

Dr. E.L. Trudeau statue. Courtesy of the Adirondack Collection, Saranac Lake Free Library P82.19

Adirondack Research Room at the Saranac Lake Free Library. Author photograph

Saranac Laboratory & Office of Historic Saranac Lake. Author photograph

More "Fond Memories of Ray Brook"

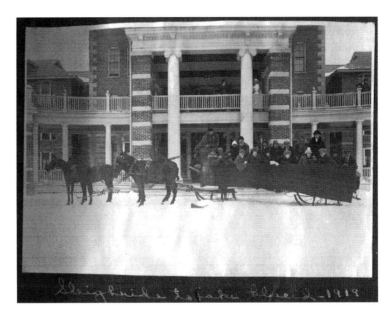

Courtesy of Helen Ryan Garlock

Courtesy of Helen Ryan Garlock

Ray Brook baseball score board, 1925. From *Woodland Whispers*, Dec. 1925

Helen Ryan, far right. Evelyn Bellak, second from right, front row. Courtesy of Helen Ryan Garlock

Did not over this morning
Diary, but went out this after
noon about 2:45 and stayed
until nearly 4. Then came in
and got ready for a walk.
Sal, Peg and I went out. Then
when we came back, we went
to the kitchen for something to
eat and met Julius. Katy just
putting the potatoes in the
steamer. She started to talk
to him and he forgot to turn
on the steam. Hence, supper
was about a half hour late.
    Harry was over tonight.
Had a nice time. Have a
date for tomorrow night.
    Got a letter from Amelia
nothing new

Sample page from Evelyn Bellak's diary. Author photo

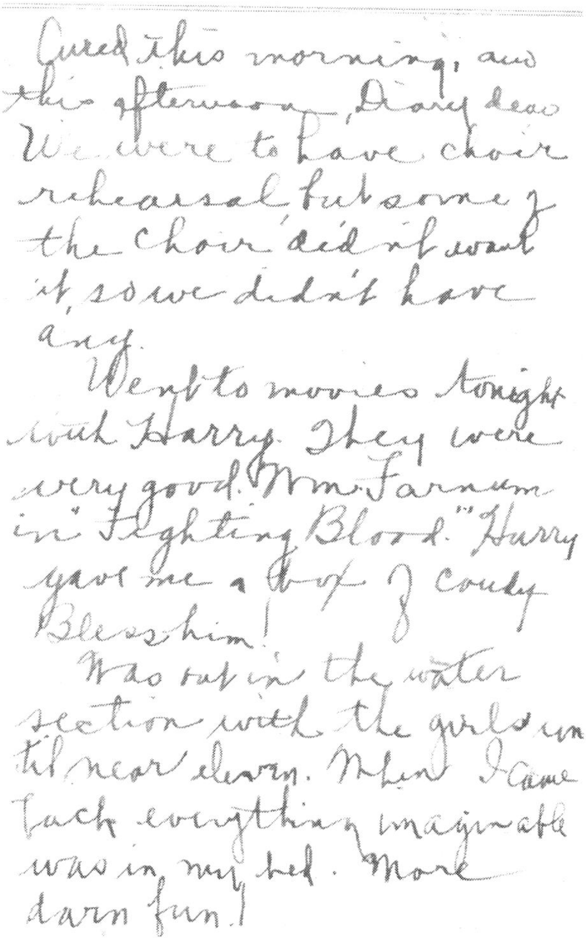

Cured this morning, and
this afternoon, Diary dear
We were to have choir
rehearsal, but some of
the choir did'nt want
it, so we did'nt have
any.

Went to movies tonight
with Harry. They were
very good. Wm. Farnum
in "Fighting Blood." Harry
gave me a box of candy
Bless him!

Was out in the water
section with the girls un
til near eleven. When I came
back everything imaginable
was in my bed. More
darn fun!

Sample page from Evelyn Bellak's diary. Author photo

Helen Ryan (left) and Evelyn Bellak. Courtesy of Helen Ryan Garlock

Acknowledgments

Helen Garlock, with the help of her daughter Margaret Garlock, gathered up and graciously allowed me to scan the Ray Brook photographs in her Aunt Helen Ryan's album along with other family photographs. Mrs. Garlock's family stories also provided details of Helen Ryan's life. Patricia Powers, though she never knew Evelyn, shared her memories from childhood of conversation about a mysterious Evelyn. Pat and her husband Bill shared what few photographs they had.

The staffs of the Local History and Genealogy Department of the Onondaga County Public Library and the Local History and Genealogy Center of the Broome County Public Library were helpful with my research on Evelyn's life outside the Ray Brook Hospital. Michele Tucker, curator of the Adirondack Research Room at the Saranac Lake Free Library, helped with illustrations. The files of the Saranac Lake Voluntary Health Association, courtesy of the staff, also provided details of Evelyn's time in Saranac Lake.

I also owe thanks to Bette M. Epstein of the New Jersey State Archives, Cara Dellatte at the Staten Island Museum, Max Hockley of the Hebrew Free Burial Association, David Cooley at the Binghamton Johnson City Monument Company, Larry A. Peck of the Charlotte County Genealogical Society, Dan Hubbs at the Saratoga Springs Public Library, and Gerald R. Smith of the Broome County Historical Society.

Very special thanks go to Don Paulson for his patient and skillful execution of my cover design. Janet Decker read and commented on the manuscript and I am sorry she passed away before seeing it published with illustrations. Caperton Tissot continually and graciously provided advice and encouragement. And my husband, Don Morgan, cheerfully became my research assistant on many exploratory ventures.

Notes

[1] The Latin plural "sanatoria" is also correct, but less commonly used today.

[2] Census records indicate that Miss Linda Cleland was "Matron" of Ray Brook State Hospital from 1910 through 1930 and "Nurse" in 1940. According to an undated typescript by Dr. Ben Fruhlinger, Linda Cleland, a former patient, was superintendent of nurses, head housekeeper, and dietician at Ray Brook.

[3] Mark Caldwell, *The Last Crusade: The War on Consumption, 1862-1954* (New York: Atheneum, 1988), 11.

[4] Edward Livingston Trudeau, *An Autobiography* (Philadelphia & New York: Lea & Ferbiger, 1916).

[5] The official name, for some period at least, was the New York State Hospital for the Treatment of Incipient Tuberculosis at Ray Brook.

[6] Kenneth W. Wright, "A History of Ray Brook State Tuberculosis Hospital," *New York State Journal of Medicine* 90, no. 8 (August 1990): 406-412.

[7] Philip P. Jacobs, *The Campaign Against Tuberculosis in the United States Including a Directory of Institutions Dealing with Tuberculosis in the United States and Canada* (New York: Russell Sage Foundation, 1908), 81.

[8] *Register of Births York County, Penna.*, December, 1901.

[9] Ward Bonsall, comp. & ed. *Handbook of Social Laws of Pennsylvania* (Pittsburgh: Associated Charities of Pittsburgh and the Philadelphia Society for Organizing Charity, 1914), 39, 42, 129.

[10] *Petition of Adolph Bellak for a Peddler's License*, filed 1891, 1893, 1894, 1897 to the Court of Quarter Sessions of York County, Pennsylvania.

[11] "Personals," *The York Press*, 3 November, 1899. A copy of the marriage certificate obtained from the New York City Department of Records and Information Services Municipal Archives confirms the date.

[12] There are discrepancies about Fanny's age and birth date in subsequent census records, but the 1870 census lists her as one year old. After the war, Fanny no longer reported to census takers that her mother was born in Germany (Prussia), probably hiding the fact because of the prejudice against Germans at the time.

[13] Lawrence J. Epstein, *At the Edge of a Dream: the Story of Jewish Immigration on New York's Lower East Side, 1880-1920* (San Francisco: Jossey-Bass, 2007), 34-37.

[14] Robert A. Divine et al, *America Past and Present* (New York: HarperCollins, 1991), 758.

[15] Epstein, 58.

[16] Ella M.E. Flick, *Dr. Lawrence F. Flick: 1856-1938* (White Haven, Pennsylvania: White Haven Sanatorium Association, 1940); *Directory of Sanatoria, Hospitals, and Day Camps for the Treatment of Tuberculosis in the United States* (New York: National Tuberculosis Association, 1918).

[17] Census data such as ages often vary a bit from one record to the next, so this number is approximate.

[18] Articles on school topics which featured Evelyn Bellak's name appeared frequently in the *Binghamton Press* and the *Endicott Record* between 1914 and 1917.

[19] Cheryl Taylor Desmond, *Shaping the Culture of Schooling: the Rise of Outcome-based Education* (Albany, New York: SUNY Press, 1996), 23.

[20] William Inglis, *George F. Johnson and His Industrial Democracy* (New York: Huntington Press, 1935), 25.

[21] Diane C. Vecchio, *Merchants, Midwives, and Laboring Women: Italian Migrants in Urban America* (University of Illinois Press, 2006), 49.

[22] *Hours of Work as Related to Output and Health of Workers: Boot and Shoe Industry* (Boston: National Industrial Conference Board, 1918), 62.

[23] Hasia R. Diner, *Erin's Daughters in America: Irish Immigrant Women in the Nineteenth Century* (Baltimore & London: The Johns Hopkins University Press, 1983), 94.

[24] Diner, 62, 98.

[25] Diner, 80, 95, 97.

[26] See Blum, Daniel C., *A Pictorial History of the Silent Screen* (New York: G.P. Putnam's Sons, 1953), available on archive.org. This book is a wonderful collection of images, organized by year of release.

[27] Saranac Lake was a part of the film industry. A pamphlet issued by the Saranac Lake Society for the Control of Tuberculosis for 1917-1918, *Interesting Facts About Saranac Lake*, calls Saranac Lake "a winter and summer mecca for motion picture companies." It goes on to say that "the outdoor scenes of many famous films were taken at Saranac Lake," especially in winter for scenes supposed to be in Alaska or Siberia.

[28] For a contemporary source on women's efforts, see Clarke, Ida Clyde *American Women and the World War* (New York: Appleton & Company, 1918), available on archive.org.

[29] The word "jigger" or "jugger" is difficult to read, but must have meant a dance.

[30] *Thirty-fifth Medical Report of the Trudeau Sanatorium and the Fifteenth Medical Supplement, for the year ending October 31, 1919,* 1.

[31] Lawrason Brown, *Rules for Recovery from Pulmonary Tuberculosis: a Layman's Handbook on Treatment* (Philadelphia and New York: Lea & Febiger, 1919), 105.

[32] Wright, 408.

[33] Cocaine was used then as an anesthetic before Novocain. It was not illegal, though the drug's addictive effect was known.

[34] Shirley Morgan, "Crafting a Cure: The Saranac Lake Study and Craft Guild Put Many Hands to Work in Sickness and Health," *Adirondack Life* XXXII No.8 (Nov/Dec 2001): 50-57, 68-69.

[35] Others coped in different ways. Two books are particularly interesting on this subject: *The Healing Woods* by Martha Reben, who went into the woods to cure with local guide Fred Rice, and *Wish I Might* by Isabel Smith, who was a patient at Trudeau Sanatorium for two decades.

[36] See Crosby, Alfred C. *America's Forgotten Epidemic: the Influenza of 1918*, 2nd ed (Cambridge & New York: Cambridge University Press, 2003.

[37] *Record Book of the Health Officer, Charles C. Trembley, Saranac Lake, New York*, May 1, 1917-?

[38] *Saranac Lake New York in the Adirondacks: Pioneer Health Resort* (Saranac Lake, New York, n.d.). This pamphlet contains the statement: "Every effort is directed toward the safeguarding and maintenance of the health of the community, and the safety of residence is amply attested by the fact that the incidences of tuberculosis among the native-born citizens is considerably less than in practically any community of equal size in this State."

[39] *Rockland Leader* 26 February, 1942, 1; "Dr. W.J. Ryan Dies Suddenly in Office of County Hospital," *The Journal* 52, no. 245 (26 February, 1942), 1.

[40] *Philadelphia Inquirer* (Undated clipping provided by Helen Garlock, estimated date: late 1930s.)

[41] *A Tuberculosis Directory Containing a List of Institutions, Associations and Other Agencies Dealing with Tuberculosis in the United States and Canada* (National Association for the Treatment and Prevention of Tuberculosis, 1916), 176.

[42] W.S. Carpenter, "Emphasizing Sanitation to School Children: How Saranac Lake Teaches Prophylaxis in the Schools—an Effective Exhibit," *Journal of the Outdoor Life* 5, no. 8 (September 1908): 282-284.

[43] *New York Times*, February 26, 1924; *Binghamton Press*, February 15, 1924.

[44] Wright, 409.

[45] There is also a disinfection date of June 15, 1929 for the Bellak Cottage at 3 Kiwassa Road, so it is possible that Fanny ran two cottages for a short time.

[46] Stella C. Norton, *Report of the Librarian* (Saranac Lake, N.Y.: 1929) 2, 3; (1930), 1.

[47] Saranac Lake Society for the Control of Tuberculosis, *Annual Report* (Saranac Lake, New York: Free Bureau of Information, April 1, 1909), 15; *Twenty-Second Annual Report of the Saranac Lake Society for the Treatment of Tuberculosis for the Year Nineteen Hundred Twenty-Eight* (Saranac Lake, New York: Free Bureau of Information, 1928), 8; *Twenty-Fourth Annual Report of the Saranac Lake Society for the Control of Tuberculosis for the Year Nineteen Hundred Thirty* (Saranac Lake, New York, 1930), 8.

[48] Philip L. Gallos, *Cure Cottages of Saranac Lake: Architecture and History of a Pioneer Health Resort* (Saranac Lake, New York, 1985), 7-21. The Endicott Johnson Cottages were located at 1 Pine Street (gone) and 45 Shepard Avenue.

[49] TB card file, Adirondack Collection, Saranac Lake Free Library.

[50] New Jersey State Vital Records, New Jersey State Archives.

[51] Albert Greaves, *A History of The Transport Service: Adventures and Experiences of United States Transports and Cruisers in the World War* (New York: George H. Doran Company, 1921), 37, 80, 168, 248.

[52] Greaves, 190.

[53] *Staten Island Advance* July 10, 1976.

[54] Margie Mason & Martha Mendoza, "When The Drugs Stop Working: First Case of Highly Drug-resistant Tuberculosis Found in U.S." *Adirondack Daily Enterprise*, Saranac Lake, New York (2 January, 2010), B1.

[55] *Trudeau Institute: Improving Health Through Medical Research* (Saranac Lake, New York: The Trudeau Institute, 2009), 6-9.

[56] http://www.historicsaranaclake.org and http://www.saranaclakelibrary.org

For Further Reading

Bonsall, Ward, comp. & ed. *Handbook of Social Laws of Pennsylvania*. Pittsburgh, Pennsylvania: Associated Charities of Pittsburgh and the Philadelphia Society for Organizing Charity, 1914.

Brown, Lawrason. *Rules for Recovery from Tuberculosis: a Layman's Handbook on Treatment*. Philadelphia and New York: Lea & Febiger, 1919.

Caldwell, Mark. *The Last Crusade: The War on Consumption, 1862-1954*. New York: Atheneum, 1988.

---. *Saranac Lake: Pioneer Health Resort*. Saranac Lake, New York: Historic Saranac Lake, 1993.

Desmond, Cheryl Taylor. *Shaping the Culture of Schooling: the Rise of Outcome-based Education*. Albany, New York: SUNY Press, 1996.

Diner, Hasia R. *Erin's Daughters in America: Irish Immigrant Women in the Nineteenth Century*. Baltimore: & London: Johns Hopkins University Press, 1983.

Divine, Robert A. et al. *America Past and Present*. 3rd ed. New York: HarperCollins, 1991.

Ellison, David L. *Healing Tuberculosis in the Woods: Medicine and Science at the End of the Nineteenth Century*. Westport, Connecticut: Greenwood Press, 1994.

Epstein, Lawrence J. *At the Edge of a Dream: the Story of Jewish Immigration on New York's Lower East Side, 1880-1920*. San Francisco: Jossey-Bass, 2007.

Flick, Ella M.E. *Dr. Lawrence F. Flick: 1856-1938*. White Haven, Pennsylvania: White Haven Sanatorium Association, 1940.

Gallos, Philip L. *Cure Cottages of Saranac Lake: Architecture and History of a Pioneer Health Resort.* Saranac Lake, New York: Historic Saranac Lake, 1985.

Greaves, Albert. *A History of the Transport Service: Adventures and Experiences of United States Transports and Cruisers in the World War.* New York: George H. Doran Company, 1921.

Inglis, William. *George F. Johnson and His Industrial Democracy.* New York: Huntington Press, 1935.

Jacobs, Philip P. *The Campaign Against Tuberculosis in the United States Including a Directory of Institutions Dealing with Tuberculosis in the United States and Canada.* New York: Russell Sage Foundation, 1908.

Mason, Jean S. "The Discourse of Disease: Patient Writing at the 'University of Tuberculosis'." *Psychoanalysis and Narrative Medicine*, ed. Rita Charon and Peter Rudnytsky. Albany, New York: SUNY Press, 2008.

National Industrial Conference Board. *Hours of Work as Related to Output and Health of Workers: Boot and Shoe Industry.* Boston, Massachusetts: National Industrial Conference Board, 1918.

Trudeau, Edward Livingston. *An Autobiography.* Philadelphia & New York: Lea & Febiger, 1916.

Index

Made in the USA
Lexington, KY
25 April 2014